SIGNIFYING NOTHING

Signifying Nothing

The Semiotics of Zero

B. (Brian) Rotman

St. Martin's Press   New York

First published in the United States of America in 1987

Printed in Great Britain

ISBN 0–312–01202–0
      0312–01203–9 (pbk)

Library of Congress Cataloging-in-Publication Data
Rotman, B. (Brian)
Signifying nothing : the semiotics of zero / Brian Rotman.
p.   cm.
Bibliography: p.
Includes index.
ISBN 0–312–01202–0 : $29.95.   ISBN 0–312–01203–9 (pbk.) : $12.95
1. Semiotics.   2. Zero (The number)   I. Title.
P99.R63   1987
001.51—dc19

                                                    87–15632
                                                    CIP

To the memory of Jill (1937–71) and to Lesley

Contents

List of Illustrations

Preface

Zero, as readers of this book will discover, is a very interesting, singular and thought provoking sign. Writing about it has proved at times to be an odd and somewhat unreal experience.

For one thing, zero is intimately connected to the idea of nothing, emptiness, the void. To write, read, talk about Nothing, or to believe in it, or to claim, as Socrates did, to know nothing, is to sit close to the obvious possibility that one is involved in the ultimate unreality of signifying not Nothing but no thing. One might think, perhaps, that in the passage of three millennia since Odysseus first used it to fool the Cyclops, by naming himself Nobody, the nature of such a one-eyed confusion has become too obvious to engender any interesting perceptions about Nothing. The hostile reception given to zero within medieval Europe and the subsequent mis-descriptions and misunderstandings of it, as a mathematical synonym for nothing, suggests otherwise and indicates that there is more to signifying nothing than meets the eye.

But, leaving Nothing and its subtleties to one side, what sort of phenomenon is zero? Does it, outside of elementary arithmetic and computer binarism, carry any contemporary intellectual or cultural charge? If titles of artefacts, intentional and proclamatory as they are, are anything to go by the answer seems to be yes. At one point during the writing of this book I felt inundated by zeros: a friend gives me a copy of a song *Down to Zero*, then a newspaper ad announces the invention and sale of *Zero Bonds*, an off-off-Broadway play called *Zero* is just closing when I arrive in New York, a novel with the title *Woman at Point Zero* is published followed by another called *Less Than Zero*, my local video shop offers me *The Zero Boys* – what is going on? Is there a zero-phenomenon out there, some actual pre-occupation with an extreme or terminal state, with the condition of being a cypher, manifested in these titles, or have I merely sensitised myself to any mention of zero, zeroing in on zero, obsessively foregrounding it out of the cultural noise? And assuming there is such a phenomenon, am I, producing this artefact and adding another item to the list, not part of it? Presumably so. In which case, how? I do not know. And do not, in any worthwhile inter-pretation of the verb, expect to know: for, whatever the phenomenon is, we (or at least I) seem to be still passing through it, and as Hegel said 'the owl of Minerva spreads its wings only with the falling of the dusk'.

In fact, the essay which follows does not address zero's contemporary significance directly, though it does I think, in a more oblique way, make it clear why somebody might consider the question worth pursuing. Neither does it address the history of zero, if by this is meant the tracing of temporal sequences of causes, effects, influences, filiations, and the like, embodied in a narrative that is intended to explain the actions and instrumentalities of historical figures and movements. Rather, the form of the essay is an archeology (in the sense that Foucault has given to the term) not an historical account: an inquiry into the nature of zero in terms of its semiotic character and the systemic, structural, paradigmatic relations it enjoys as a *sign* among other signs and signifying patterns. This means that I discuss, as indeed does Foucault in *The Order of Things*, patterns of similitude, homology, structural identity, parallelism, and the like between various different signifying systems and codes such as mathematics, painting, money, and, to a lesser extent, written texts. But the overall divisions and phases of semiotic space which emerge in the present account do not map in any very productive way onto the *epistemes* into which Foucault cuts the field of historical data. In view of this I have, in the interests of clarity, directness and a certain rhetorical simplicity, followed a path of my own through zero and avoided comparison with the findings, though obviously not the method, of his pioneering work.

This book started life as a lecture given originally at Cornell University and then at various institutions both here and in the United States. It would be impossible to thank the many audience members for their helpful comments, responses and criticisms, but among them I owe particular debts of gratitude to Neil Hertz, Marty Roth, Anthony Kerrigan for their suggestions; also to Roy Porter for the usefulness of his comments on an early draft of the book, and especially to Norman Bryson for his sympathetic comprehending of two versions of the manuscript and the generous encouragement that came with it.

London   BRIAN ROTMAN

0
Opening

The first purpose of this book is to portray the introduction of the mathematical sign zero into Western consciousness in the thirteenth century as a major signifying event, both in its own right within the writing of numbers and as the emblem of parallel movements in other sign systems.

Specifically, I shall argue that certain crucial changes in the codes of number, visual depiction, and monetary exchange that occurred as part of the discontinuity in Western culture known as the Renaissance – the introduction of *zero* in the practice of arithmetic, the *vanishing point* in perspective art, and *imaginary money* in economic exchange – are three isomorphic manifestations, different, but in some formal semiotic sense equivalent models, of the same signifying configuration. Zero is to number signs, as the vanishing point is to perspective images, as imaginary money is to money signs. In all three codes the sign introduced is a sign about signs, a *meta-sign*, whose meaning is to indicate, via a syntax which arrives with it, the absence of certain other signs. Further, I shall argue that the shifts that take place within these codes – from Roman to Hindu numerals, from the images of gothic art to those of perspectival painting, from gold coinage to the use of imaginary bank money – exhibit parallel patterns of semiotic disruption.

Despite its formal equivalence with the vanishing point and imaginary money, zero has a primary status, a privileged claim to attention, on several counts. First, and most simply, the introduction of zero occurred earlier than changes in the signs of painting and money and can therefore be seen in a relatively pristine state uncomplicated by historical relations it might have with these other changes. Secondly, zero is epistemologically rudimentary: not only in the sense that mathematics claims to provide objective, historically invariant, empirically unfalsifiable 'truth', thus making its signs more culturally and logically naked, transparent, and parsimonious than other signs, but in the immediately practical sense that counting is a simpler more primitive semiotic activity than viewing a painting, and number signs are a necessary cognitive precursor of any kind of money transaction. And finally, zero's connection, obscure but undeniable, to the much older and more deeply embedded idea of 'nothing' indicates that questions about its introduction be phrased in very general terms. One can ask: what is the impact on a written code when a sign for Nothing, or more precisely when a

1

sign for the absence of other signs, enters its lexicon? What can be said through the agency of such a sign that could not be said, was unsayable, without it?

To suggest that the Hindu number sign zero might be emblematic of fundamental changes in the signs of painting and money, and to assert that in any case it can be seen as the paradigm and prototype of these changes, is to claim for zero an exalted role: an intellectual significance and status in conflict with its banal, everyday, unspectacular appearance as a constituent of the decimal notation for numbers or of the binary system on which computer languages are based. Indeed, even to speak of zero as the origin of a large-scale change within *mathematics* seems to be at variance with how mathematicians and historians of mathematics construe the matter.

Thus, although we learn from historical accounts that zero was introduced into medieval Europe with great misunderstanding and difficulty, that it was unknown either to the Romans or the classical Greeks, that equivalent versions of it were used and obviously understood by both the Babylonian mathematicians of the Hellenistic period and the pre-Columbian Mayas, we are not presented with any sense of the semiotic difficulty – the peculiar, enigmatic, and profoundly abstract challenge that zero presented, as a *sign*. A sign, moreover, whose connection to 'nothing', the void, the place where no thing is, makes it the site of a systematic ambiguity between the absence of 'things' and the absence of signs, and the exemplar, as we shall see, of a semiotic phenomenon whose importance lies far beyond notation systems for numbers.

Again, though mathematicians are obliged to make certain concessions to the special status of zero and its derivatives – the empty set, for example, is given a special kind of definition and is acknowledged to play a unique and privileged role as the origin of the hierarchy of infinite sets within which all of mathematics is supposed to take place – they push the matter as a question about the nature of *signs* no further. Perhaps this is because the majority of mathematicians, as well as historians of the subject, are philosophical realists, in the sense that they take mathematics to be about 'things' – numbers, points, lines, spaces, functions, and so on – that are somehow considered to be external and prior to mathematical activity; things which though formulated in terms of mathematical symbols, have none the less a pre-mathematical existence that cannot be accounted for solely in terms of the signs mathematicians themselves produce. In the course of this book I will reject such a view, and suggest that this insistence on the priority of certain 'things' to mathematical signs is a misconception, a referentialist misreading, of the nature of written signs; a misconception not, by any means, peculiar to mathematics, but one repeated for visual and monetary signs through the natural but mistaken notion that a painting is simply a depiction and money a representation of some prior visual or economic reality.

Focusing on the nature and status of zero, and likewise the vanishing point and imaginary money, as certain kinds of creative originating meta-signs leads inevitably to the question of origins, to the manner in which signs are produced and created. Signs, meta-signs and the codes in which they operate do not arise and exist by themselves, they are not given as formal objects in some abstract already present space. They are *made* and remade repeatedly whether spoken, counted, written, painted, exchanged, gestured, inscribed, or transacted, they come into being and then persist by virtue of human agency, through the continued activity of interpretation-making sign-using subjects. Such subjects are not to be identified with individuals, with persons who feel themselves to be authors and recipients of sign utterances; rather, they are semiotic capacities – public, culturally constituted, historically identifiable *forms* of utterance and reception which codes make available to individuals.

The picture presented here will, therefore, elaborate on the signifying acts initiated by certain specific semiotic subjects – the one-who-counts, the one-who-sees, and the one-who-buys-and-sells – and on the distinction made for these subjects between being an external agent and an internal recipient of signification; a distinction which though a graspable as a felt, experienced difference, is notoriously difficult to convey by the subject himself. Thus, St Augustine likened the difficulty of separating signs from signs about signs, of distinguishing between talk and talk about talk, to a physical misperception:

> Discussing words with words is as entangled as interlocking and rubbing the fingers with the fingers, where it may scarcely be distinguished, except by the one who does it, which fingers itch and which give aid to the itching.
>
> (St Augustine, *De Magistro in Gribble, 1968*, p. 98)

Clearly, a discourse interested in illuminating the relation of signs to meta-signs, has to go beyond St Augustine's image of a private self in a state of bodily confusion between inner proprioception and outer perception, and replace it by an observable relation between publicly signifying agencies, between, that is, semiotic subjects.

One consequence of employing a vocabulary of semiotic, as opposed to individual, subjects will be that the failure to distinguish between inner perception (self as author of signs) and outer perception (author as subject of signs), between words and words about words, will be seen not as an error, a confusion to be clarified, but as the inevitable result of a systematic linguistic process which elides this very difference. A process whereby meta-signs are denied their status as signs of signs and appear as mere signs: zero becomes just another number among the infinity of numbers, the vanishing point appears indistinguishable from all the many other depicted locations within a painting, imaginary money is treated as simply more money. In this naturalisation of meta-signs into signs – obviously akin to figures of speech dying and becoming literal – it becomes necessary, if one is to explicate what it means for a sign to signify other signs, to retrieve the fate of the absented subject. For it is the manner of its absence, the sort of naturalisation it is subjected to, which sets the stage for the emergence of a secondary formation to the original meta-sign.

Specifically, I shall show how zero gives rise at the end of the sixteenth century to a semiotic closure of itself, namely the algebraic variable; likewise the vanishing point will be seen to engender a closure, during the seventeenth century, in the form of the multi-perspective image; and similarly imaginary money finds its semiotic closure in the emergence of paper money at the end of the seventeenth century. Moreover, we shall see that each of these new signs is itself a certain kind of meta-sign in relation to the system that spawns it; a meta-sign that requires the formulation of a new sign-using agency, a secondary subjectivity, in order to be recognised. It will be shown that this new capacity, a self-conscious subject of a subject, a *meta-subject*, is at the centre of major eruptions within very different sign systems of the sixteenth and seventeenth century. These major eruptions were, in mathematics, the invention of algebra by Vieta; in painting, the self-conscious image created by Vermeer and Velasquez; in the text, the invention of the autobiographical written self by Montaigne; in economics, the creation of paper money by gold merchants in London.

All these signs, the original meta-signs as well as their closures, are structured around the notion of an absence, in the sense of a signified non-presence of certain signs; a notion that occurs in stark and prototypical form in the case of zero, which presents itself as the absence of *anything*, as 'nothing': the statements '$1 - 1 = 0$' and 'one taken away from one is nothing' are, in common parlance, read as translations of each other. Thus, in order to pursue the historical impact of zero in terms of the resistance it encountered as a sign, one has to ask questions about what 'nothing' was supposed to signify within European intellectual discourse. How, for example, was Nothing cognised within the Christian orthodoxy which dominated this discourse and in the classical Greek conception that underpinned it? If medieval hostility to zero rested on a Christian antagonism to 'nothing', since to talk of something being no-thing, to give credence to that which was not and could not be in God's world, was to risk blasphemy or heresy, then it must also be said that this antagonism was itself ambiguous and unstable. Christian adherence to the classical Greek denial of 'the void' was in conflict with its acceptance of the account in Genesis in which the universe was created out of 'nothing'.

Notions of Nothing and responses to what it – and its dialectical opposites of All, Infinity, the Cosmos – could be taken to signify in sixteenth- and seventeenth-century European thought were not, however, confined to the arena of theological and doctrinal dispute. *Ex nihilo nihil* (nothing will come from nothing) was a classical maxim that acted as a starting point for a great deal of rhetorical and metaphysical speculation that had ultimately very little to do with Christianity. Nowhere is this more dramatically the case than in Shakespeare's profoundly non-Christian play, *King Lear*. A work which not only explicitly and obviously concerns itself with a certain sort of horror that comes from nothing, but which less obviously, although as I shall demonstrate equally explicitly, locates the origin of this horror in the secular effect and mercantile purport of the sign zero.

The assertion that zero and zero-like signs permeate several, very different, signifying codes and artefacts of the Renaissance is not unexpected if one thinks of changes in these codes in historically materialist terms: the historical emergence of mercantile capitalism rode on the vector of trade, business, commerce, finance, money. And money required a system of writing, which included book-keeping and calculation, to enable it to function as an international medium of exchange. It was precisely to meet this need that double-entry book-keeping and Hindu numerals, both written in terms of zero, were introduced in Italy at the beginning of the Renaissance in the thirteenth century. Zero then was a principal element of Renaissance, that is to say mercantile capitalism's, systems of writing from the beginning.

After mercantile, industrial, monopoly capitalism comes the most recent form, financial capitalism, dedicated to the buying and selling of money and all the financial instruments created and sustained by money. Financial capitalism operates through an instantaneous global market whose book-keeping and calculation needs are met by computer. Computers, as is well known, communicate with themselves, each other, and with human beings through sequences of 0s and 1s. Now the presence of 0 here is no accident. Much can be made of the relation between it and the Boolean algebra which governs how computers do what they do. But an analysis of Boolean logic is too esoteric for the scope of this present book and too technical a route to zero's semiotic involvement within financial capitalism. Capitalism's way with signs is through money, so it is more useful to put the question directly and ask: what sort of money sign has financial capitalism engendered?

The answer will be a type of sign that replaces the familiar modern conception of money, that is paper money whose value is its promise of redemption by gold or silver, by a money note which promises nothing but an identical copy of itself; and which determines its value, what it signifies as a sign, in the form of a certain kind of self-reference. This new type of money sign which, for reasons which will emerge, I call *xenomoney*, will be seen to disrupt and displace the code of paper money in a way that mimics the replacement of the code of Roman numerals achieved by zero.

The new global order of money signs represented by xenomoney is a contemporary economic construction, a current achievement of Western capitalist culture. Now since money is the dominating source of 'value', the image of images, the only absolute given signifying credence in this culture, the question arises whether there ought to be isomorphic patterns, changes parallel to that experienced by money signs, within other contemporary codes. Should one expect to see similar disruptions in the written codes of mathematics, music, visual repesentation, or the written word? I shall respond only to the last of these questions by giving a brief and oblique des-c iption of what, according to the philosopher Jacques Derrida, we must in future mean by 'the text'.

1

Number, Vision, Money

ZERO

It is clear that zero is the true and natural beginning.
(Stevin, 1958, vol. IIB, p. 499)

Zero is not an absence, not nothing, not the sign of a thing, not a simple exclusion. If the natural numbers are signs, it is a signifier. It is not an integer, but a meta-integer, a rule about integers and their relationships.
(Wilden, 1972, p. 188)

Since nothing falls under the concept 'not identical with itself', I define nought as follows: 0 is the number which belongs to the concept 'not identical with itself'.
(Frege, 1974, p. 87)

Zero understood as a number, which assigns to the subsuming concept the lack of an object, is as such a thing – *the first non-real thing in thought.*
Miller, 1977–8, p. 30)

The mathematical sign we know as zero entered European consciousness with difficulty and incomprehension. It appears to have originated some 1300 years ago in central India as the distinguishing element in the now familiar Hindu system of numerals. From there it was actively transmitted and promulgated by Arab merchants; so that by the tenth century it was in widespread use throughout the Arab Mediterranean. Between the tenth and the thirteenth century the sign stayed within the confines of Arab culture, resisted by Christian Europe, and dismissed by those whose function it was to handle numbers as an incomprehensible and unnecessary symbol.

During the fourteenth century, with the emergence of mercantile capitalism in Northern Italy, the handling of numbers passed from church educated clerks immersed in Latin to merchants, artisan-scientists, architects, educated in the vernacular for whom arithmetic was an essential prerequisite for trade and technology; with the result that the texts of those who had long been advocating the introduction of Arab mathematics and in par-

7

ticular Hindu numerals, such as Fibonacci in his treatise *Liber Abaci* of 1202, became increasingly influential. The central role occupied by double-entry book-keeping (principle of the zero balance) and the calculational demands of capitalism broke down any remaining resistance to the 'infidel symbol' of zero, and ensured that by the early seventeenth century Hindu numerals had completely replaced Roman ones as the dominant mode of recording and manipulating numbers throughout Europe.

Given that the Hindu system offered from the very beginning of the tenth century a clear, efficient, easily learned method for writing numbers and handling calculations (or so it seems now after long familiarity with it), the nature of the resistance the sign 0 encountered for several centuries can be queried. What, from a semiotic point of view, might have been so difficult and alien about the number zero? One answer would be that zero, being somehow about 'nothing', became therefore the object of a hostility to 'nothing' already entrenched within Christian orthodoxy. I shall return to this answer and the nature of this hostility later. For the present I want to focus on the question in terms of the purely formal properties of zero as a signifying item within the decimal notation for numbers.

Though there are many different ways of talking about the mathematical concept of number, there is in all discussions a *sine qua non*: the activity of counting. It seems to be impossible to imagine any picture, characterisation, elaboration, or description of numbers that does not rely on a prior conceptual familiarity (whether this be explicitly formulated or assumed as background knowledge) with the process of counting. And since counting requires the repetition of an identical act, it is impossible to imagine the creation of numbers – as a mathematical activity of writing signs – without invoking characteristic patterns of concatenated marks such as:

1, 11, 111, 1111, 11111, 111111, 1111111, etc.

formed by iterating the operation of making some, indeed any, particular mark.

These patterns acquire significance as the elements of an ordered sequence of mathematical signs, as soon as the 'etc.' symbol is interpreted as a mathematical imperative, a command addressed to a subject, instructing him to enact the recursive rule: copy previous inscription then add another mark; the rule, that is, which means continue counting.

Seen in this way, numbers become *potentia*, theoretical possibilities of sign production, the imaginable signifying acts of a subject-who-counts. In a strict sense, therefore, they are not to be identified with the signs 1, 11, 111, etc. Rather, these signs are records left by the one-who-counts, particular representations of numbers recorded in a written medium.

However, the historical precedence of signs such as these – in the form of notches, scratches, and tally-marks – over all known systems of numerical

notation allows us to consider them as a kind of proto-number; thus sim-
plifying the discussion of numerals, since any system of names for numbers,
such as the Roman or the Hindu system, can be taken as a systematic rewrit-
ing of the signs 1, 11, 111, etc. As such, each system of numerals arises as a
different solution, with its own desiderata and semiotic priorities, to the
same fundamental problem: how to re-convey, through a system of signs
which preserves the different numerical identities of the individual proto-
numbers, the activity of the counting subject.

The principal semiotic feature of the proto-numbers is the iconic manner
in which they function: each constituent sign, each '1' in the typical proto-
number 111. . .1, has for its signified a 'unit' which records a single act within
the process of counting, with a plurality of such acts being recorded by a *corresponding* plurality of signs. Moreover, because they are identical and
interchangeable, the constituent signs combine commutatively. The order
in which they are written is immaterial. Any system of numerals will,
therefore, introduce abbreviations, conventions of syntax and grammar,
designed to de-iconise the proto-numbers. With this in mind let us compare
Roman and Hindu numerals.

In its earliest form the Roman system of numerals was based on the signs
I, V, X, L, (, I), (I) for one, five, ten, fifty, one hundred, five hundred, one
thousand respectively. The introduction of printing in the fifteenth century
brought modifications: the sign '(' became C, the sign '1)' became D, and (I)
became M, thus masking the recursive, exponential facility the system
possesses whereby ((I)) was ten thousand, (((I))) was a hundred thousand,
and so on. By writing these original signs alongside each other, with the convention that concatenation was to be interpreted as addition, so that for
example MMMMDCCLXXXVI represented 4 thousands plus 7 hundreds
plus 8 tens plus 6 units, the Roman system was capable of producing a
numeral for any number that its users could conceive.

Despite its abbreviations, the Roman way of notating numbers, like those
languages that express the plural by repeating the singular, did not detach
itself from the iconic mode, as is witnessed in the writing of MMMMMMMMM
for 9 thousand and so on. (Subsequent modifications introduced an order
into the syntax through the subtractive principle whereby IX represented 9
and so on, leaving iconicity to remain in II for 2, III for 3, IIII for 4, MMMM
for 4 thousand, and so on.) Independently of these features the system's use
of the operator (–) was confined to powers of ten – ((I)) was permitted but
((II)) was not – so that while one million was written as ((((I)))), it would
have been necessary (had Roman arithmeticians ever considered the
number) to resort to iconic duplication and write ((((I))))((((I)))) for two
million, and so on. The result of this curtailment in the use of the operator (–)
was that the syntactic structure of Roman numerals assumed an arbitrary,
heterogenous, and locally complex character.

One consequence of this *ad hoc* syntax was an overcomplicated grammar:

performing all but the most elementary *calculations* with Roman numerals assumes a laborious, byzantine, impractical character. Ordinary multiplications, for example, require such intricate sign manipulations as to render the Roman system virtually unworkable as a computational medium. And indeed, throughout its history there is no evidence that the system of Roman numerals was used or ever intended to be used for calculation. Instead, calculations were carried out, not as manipulations of written numerals, but as operations on the beads of a counting-board or *abacus*.

An abacus, as a machine which keeps track of the process of counting, consists of an array of grooves or wires determining an ascending series of rows on which counters or tokens are positioned. Tokens on the bottom row represent units, the next row tens, the next hundreds, and so on. Additionally, intermediate rows are possible with a token representing a 5, or a 50, or a 500, and so on. The state of the abacus – the configuration of positions occupied by its tokens – can express and be determined by a unique numeral. Thus, the numeral MMMMDCCLXXXVI would correspond to the state:

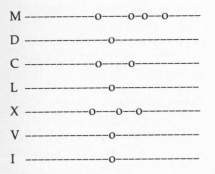

In a calculation, the tokens would be manipulated according to the rule that two tokens on an intermediate row or five on any other row would be replaced by a token on the next row up; the result of the calculation being the final state of the abacus. (see Illustration 1).

In the period between the tenth and thirteenth centuries the *abacists*, who wrote Roman numerals but calculated with the abacus, were in conflict with the *algorists*, who both recorded and calculated with Hindu numerals. For the abacists what was objectionable about the algorists' procedure was not any rejection of the notational principles associated with the abacus, since if intermediate rows are ignored, Hindu numerals correspond just as naturally to the state of the abacus as Roman ones; indeed, the very form of the correspondence, whereby the state

Illustration 1 Gregor Reisch: *Margarita Philosophica*. The two forms of calculation contrasted, with Boethius representing the use of Hindu numerals and Pythagoras that of the abacus.

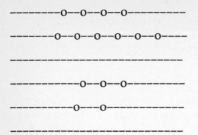

is written as 460320, seems so natural as to make it plausible that the origin of Hindu numerals was in the writing down of abacus states. (A suggestion made indirectly by Needham (1959, p. 11) where he remarks that zero's etymological connection to 'emptiness' might be related to the empty spaces that occur in the abacus.) Indeed, the difficulty for the abacists lay in the algorists' treatment of empty rows, and the effect this had on calculations. For the abacist, the occurrence of a row with no tokens on it, far from presenting any special problem, made it easier to write down the state of the abacus, since to do so fewer signs were required. Unlike the case with Hindu numerals, no Roman numeral ever had to register the *absence* of some particular power of ten.

The fundamental obstacle for the abacists was, of course, the peculiar use of the zero sign by the algorists; a sign which affected values of numerals wherever it occurred but had no value itself, and which appeared as a number in calculations though it answered to no positive or real quantity.

The etymology of zero, via 'cypher' from the Hindu *sunya* (= void), clearly recalls its intimate and long-standing connection both to the idea of an empty meaningless character and to the notion of 'nothing' or no thing. In any event, there is no doubt that, as a numeral, the mathematical sign zero points to the absence of certain other mathematical signs, and not to the non-presence of any real 'things' that are supposedly independent of or prior to signs which represent them. At any place within a Hindu numeral the presence of zero declares a specific absence: namely, the absence of the signs 1, 2, . . . ,9 at that place. Zero is thus a sign about signs, a meta-sign, whose meaning as a name lies in the way it indicates the absence of the names 1, 2, . . . , 9.

If zero is a name it is also none the less a *number*. Here, too, its meaning is to indicate the absence of mathematical signs; specifically, the absence of the proto-numbers 1, 11, 111, 1111, etc. Such an absence – in effect the potential, yet to be realised, presence of any positive integer – can be construed in two different ways depending on whether the numbers produced by counting are seen as cardinals or ordinals. If we interpret counting cardinally, then the proto-numbers appear as signs that iconically mark out fixed pluralities via a tallying procedure which assigns the typical proto-number 11 . . . 1 to a *corresponding* plurality of counted objects; a process that makes zero the cardinal number – nought – of the empty plurality. In other words, zero marks the theoretical limit of this sort of one to one correspondence; the point at which a counting subject, instead of tallying idealised marks to objects, must signal the complete absence of any such corresponding mark. If counting is interpreted ordinally, the proto-numbers 1, 11, 111, etc. appear as records which mark out by iconic repetition the sequence of stages occupied by a counting subject. Zero then represents the starting point of the process; indicating the virtual presence of the *counting subject* at the place where that subject begins the whole activity of traversing what will become a sequence of counted positions. It is presumably this trace of subjectivity, pointed to but absent, that Hermann Weyl (1949, p. 75) was referring to when, in his constructivist account of the mathematical subject, he characterised the origin of coordinates, represented by 0 on the line and by (0,0) in the plane and so on, as the 'necessary residue of ego extinction'.

Thus, zero points to the absence of certain signs either by connoting the origin of quantity, the empty plurality, or by connoting the origin of ordering, the position which excludes the possibility of predecessors. These connotations constitute zero's role as a meta-sign formulated in terms of, but separate from and exterior to, the proto-numbers. But zero also occurs within the domain of 'number' in direct arithmetical contact with ordinary numbers. In such equations as $0 = 0, 1 - 1 = 0, 3 + 0 = 4 - 1, 3(2 - 2) = 0$, and so on, zero appears explicitly as a number among numbers, having the same status as, operating on the same plane as, and interchangeable with, the other numbers.

It is this double aspect of zero, as a sign inside the number system and as a meta-sign, a sign-about-signs outside it, that has allowed zero to serve as the site of an ambiguity between an empty character (whose covert mysterious quality survives in the connection between 'cyphers' and secret codes), and a character for emptiness, a symbol that signifies nothing.

Finally, one can see that zero, by signifying the absence of signs, facilitates the lifting of calculations from the abacus onto paper; the shifting, that is, from 'counter-casting' with physical number tokens, to 'pen-reckoning' with the written Hindu numerals themselves. To move from abacus to paper is to shift from a *gestural* medium (in which physical movements are given ostensively and transiently in relation to an external apparatus) to a *graphic* medium (in which permanent signs, having their origin in these movements, are subject to a syntax given independently of any physical interpretation). Thus, the absence of tokens on an abacus row will be *used*. It will have meaning in use: material, gestural, computational, significance within the course of an abacus calculation, but it will not figure as a sign in any Roman numeral description of the abacus. It will never be *mentioned*, as it must be if it is to become an explicit object of graphic manipulation.

In short: as a numeral within the Hindu system, indicating the absence of any of the numerals 1,2,3,4,5,6,7,8,9, zero is a sign about names, a meta-numeral; and as a number declaring itself to be the origin of counting, the trace of the one-who-counts and produces the number sequence, zero is a meta-number, a sign indicating the whole potentially infinite progression of integers.

THE VANISHING POINT

The vanishing point is the anchor of a system which *incarnates* the viewer, renders him tangible and corporeal, a measurable, and above all a visible object in a world of absolute visibility.

(Bryson, 1983, p. 106)

This singular moment [Brunelleschi's demonstration] marks the realization of one of the most profound ideas in all of world history: the perceptual 'truth' of linear perspective.

(Edgerton, 1976, p. 125)

In 1425, a century or so before Galileo is said to have demonstrated linear acceleration by dropping his celebrated cannonball from the tower in Pisa, the architect Brunelleschi held up a mirror in an equally momentous and dramatic experiment in front of the Baptistery in Florence to demonstrate the illusionistic power of linear perspective.

With the Baptistery directly in front of him, what did Brunelleschi do? Imagine a square canvas with a painting on it depicting the scene in front of you. At a certain point in the canvas a pinhole is made. Would it be possible, by looking through the pinhole from *behind* the canvas at a square mirror placed to block the scene, to see, reflected in the mirror, a perfect copy of the scene (see Illustration 2)?

Because mirrors reverse left and right, such an effect, for it to work at all, requires the scene being viewed to be symmetrical about a vertical axis; a condition satisfied by the view of the Baptistery Brunelleschi chose to confront. It also requires that the set-up be exactly right: that distances between canvas, mirror, and scene be in the correct geometric proportion. More particularly, the demonstration rests in a critical way on the precise nature of the visual coding used to represent the scene on the canvas. What Brunelleschi's experiment showed was that if the depiction was carried out according to a certain systematic procedure, subsequently codified as the rules of artificial or linear perspective, then indeed there *was* a position on

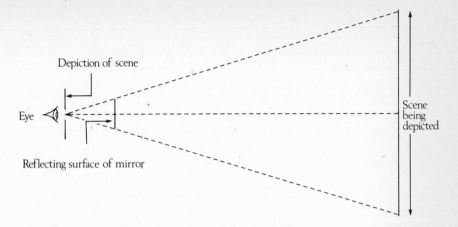

Illustration 2 Diagram of Brunelleschi's experiment. Cross-section of optic cone whose vertex is situated at pinhole through which mirror is monocularly seen.

the canvas for a pinhole through which the required illusory mirror image could be seen (see Illustration 3).

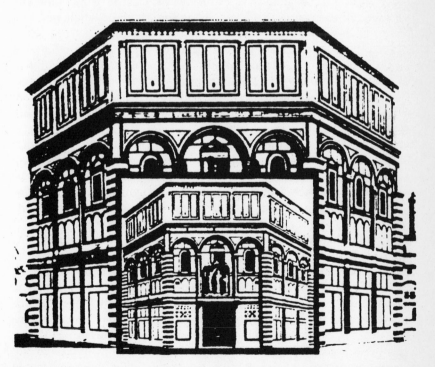

Illustration 3 Simulation of Brunelleschi's experiment. Simulated mirror view through pinhole of depicted image of Baptistery set against Baptistery itself.

Within a short time the effect so palpably demonstrated by Brunelleschi was theorised into a system by Alberti, and then clarified, developed, extended, and modified by (among others) Piero della Francesca, Uccello, Leonardo in Italy, and by van Eyck, Viator (with qualification), Dürer and de Vries further afield. The result was the emergence of a code of visual depiction that has dominated all subsequent Western attempts to represent the look of solid, occupiable space by means of a two-dimensional image.

The technical background to the emergence of Brunelleschi's demonstration, considered as a two-dimensional illusory presentation of space, contained several strands. In terms of physical artefacts these were: the growing introduction of flat (as opposed to convex) mirrors and the optical theories they gave rise to; the rediscovery of Ptolemaic map-making with its central idea of the projection of territory onto a flat surface; the long-known but new found attraction of the *camera obscura* with its ability to transfer illusory, life like portrayals of visual reality onto any surface. The relative importance of these artefacts, either as models or as indirect causative influences on the emergence of perspectival seeing, is a subject for historical dispute and does not, in any case, concern us. This is because we are interested in the code of perspectival art purely abstractly, as a formal method, a semiotic system of rules for generating an infinity of picture signs: each of which offers an illusionistic representation, artificially organised around a single point, of some real or imagined visual scene.

This being so, there is, however, one historical aspect of the system that does require elaboration, if only because it is a constituent of the system itself: the centrality and practical importance of *proportion*, the growing preoccupation with arithmetical ratios, among the merchants, architects, artisan scientists, and painters who formed the audience for Brunelleschi's demonstration.

Baxandall (1972) describes how problems relating to proportion dominated the educational curriculum, aesthetic framework, and cognitive style of the period in which Brunelleschi and Alberti formulated their ideas. The importance of such problems, if not their origin, stemmed from the exigency of mercantile capitalism: the pressing need to conduct transactions between countries and city states each possessing a different systems of weights, volumes, measurement, and currency. This required a simple, instantly applicable way of handling such exchanges within an arithmetical formalism; a formalism which at its simplest level – where it was called 'the rule of three' – answers the question: if the proportion of A to B is the same as that of C to D, and if A, B, C are given, then what is D? The 'rule of three' – essentially no more than equality between arithmetic ratios – was, as Baxandall well illustrates, elevated into a central, universally taught, cognitive principle that imposed itself on trade, architectural design, and painting.

Clearly, the rule of three' is an important facilitating tool for a system of painting basing itself on proportional enlargements and foreshortenings of the visible world. But proportion and the ability to instantly calculate it do not by themselves add up to a system of linear perspective: one also needs a point of projection from which all ratios are determined. In fact, in the absence of any such external originating point, proportional ratios occur spatially in the form of similar triangles within Euclidean geometry. And Euclidean space – in which there are no signs for isolated points other than those that are either posited outright or exist through the intersection of figures – is radically different from a projected, coordinated space; a space in which every position is signifiable in relation to the horizon and centric ray as axes and the vanishing point as origin of coordinates. (Indeed, the mathematical space appropriate to perspectival images is that of projective geometry which, in order to study the effect upon plane figures of changing the position of the point of projection, postulates a point at infinity as its origin.)

The procedure for making a perspective painting is simple enough: the scene, a fragment of the visible world, is to be viewed framed as if through a fixed rectangular window. To depict the scene the painter has to create a screen which, if placed filling the window, would at least in principle fool the eye into the belief that it was witnessing the original scene. In order to make the appropriate counterfeit image the painter imagines lines in space connecting objects to his eye; where these lines intersect the screen he makes his marks (see Illustration 4). If he keeps his viewing eye always in the same spot, then these marks will be signs which represent, continuously point for point, the surfaces of things within the visible world.

Among these signs there is one, situated on the horizon, with a uniquely privileged status: the method of perspective demands that while lines parallel to the screen are represented by parallel lines (transversals) which recede to the horizon line, those witnessed as perpendicular to the screen are represented by a cone of lines convergent to a single point. The sign occupying this point – the point where Brunelleschi must have made his pinhole – is known as the *vanishing point* or 'point of flight'. And it is this sign which organises the perspectival image for the spectator.

The transversals, by receding away from the spectator, mark out the depth of the pictorial space. Extended in the opposite direction out of the frame of the picture towards the viewer, they allow the ground on which the depicted figures and buildings stand to merge with that of the spectator. The spectator has the illusion of being drawn frontally into the picture towards the vanishing point (see Illustration 5).

Many early Renaissance painters, as if to emphasise the essential otherness and exteriority of this location, placed the vanishing point inside a hole: a framed opening, such as a door, a window, a mirror, or even another painting, within the visual scene. This had the effect of doubling the pull

Illustration 4 Albrecht Dürer: the designer of the sitting man.

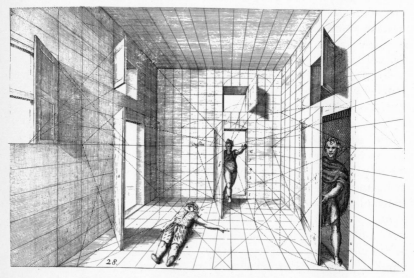

Illustration 5 Jan V. de Vries: *Perspective*, plate 28.

exerted by the vanishing point on the spectator, and at the same time, by invoking the potentially unlimited iteration of a frame within a frame, of pushing the vanishing point out to an infinite, unreal, numinous distance.

What is exceptional about the vanishing point in relation to other locations within the picture is its dual semiotic character. Like zero it plays a very specific double role. Internally, as a sign among signs, it acts as a depictive sign on the same plane as other such signs. Accordingly, like them it represents a definite location within the real physical scene witnessed through the window frame; a location that by being infinitely far in the distance, however, is unoccupiable by a person or indeed any physical object. Externally, the vanishing point is in a meta-linguistic relation to these signs, since its function is to organise them into a coherent unified image. Its meaning, in other words, can only be retrieved from the process of depiction itself, from the way the original subjective act of witnessing is represented via the rules of perspective as an image addressed to a spectator.

One can observe how the vanishing point functions as a visual zero facilitating the generation of an infinity of perspective images as zero generates an infinity of Hindu numerals. And just as zero mediates between two different subjectivities – facilitating the transition from the gestural to the graphic subject – so the vanishing point, ambiguous between its lingual meaning as an internal sign, and its external, meta-lingual sense, offers the spectator the possibility of momentarily becoming, via a thought experiment, the artist. By looking through one eye, from a certain point on the centric ray (the line through the vanishing point perpendicular to the plane of the painting), the spectator can mirror the artist's monocular witnessing and painting from what he imagines to be the corresponding point within the depicted scene. Thus, the vanishing point, by marking the artist's horizon point, that is the spot he faces on the horizon of the scene he depicts, becomes the mark of the spectator's horizon point. The spectator sees from the artist's 'point of view'.

We can see from this, as Brunelleschi so spectacularly dramatised, that the vanishing point acts as a mirror, reflecting back to the spectator an imagined version of himself, a fictive visual self in the guise of the artist (see Illustration 6).

Each image within the code of perspectival art thus offers the spectator the possibility of objectifying himself, the means of perceiving himself, from the outside, as a unitary seeing subject, since each image makes a deictic declaration: this is how I see (or would see) some real or imagined scene from this particular spot at this particular instant in time. Being able to signify such a particularised individuality equips the perspective code with the visual equivalent of a demonstrative pronoun, allowing the code to deal in messages whose interpretation requires the active presence of a physically located, corporeal individual who has a 'point of view'. Presumably, the very idea of a subject having a point of view, within a discourse

Illustration 6   Jan V. de Vries: *Perspective*, plate 30.

in the figurative sense, has its origin in the system of mirror depiction introduced by Brunelleschi.

In any event, just as the fundamentally iconic basis of Roman numerals is foreign to zero's meta-linguistic capacity to connote the trace of the one-who-counts, so the iconic images of Gothic art are silent about the nature of visual authorship and exclude the possibility of signifying demonstratively. What gives a Gothic panel its unity, its visuo-conceptual coherence, allowing different places to coexist and different historical realities to impinge on each other, is not some visual mode particularised in an individual artist/spectator, but the all-seeing timeless, spaceless eye of God.

In the fifteenth century this divine eye was vividly concretised by N. de Cusa (1928) in *The Vision of God or the Icon*; a book that de Cusa, a cardinal of the church, sent to accompany the gift of a devotional artefact, a painted portrait, which offered the brethren of a monastic order an 'easy path unto mystical theology' (p. 1):

> If I strive in human fashion to transport you to things divine, I must needs use a comparison of some kind. Now among men's works I have found no image better suited to our purpose than that of an image which is omnivoyant – its face, by the painter's cunning art, being made to appear as though looking on all around it. There are many excellent examples of such faces ... Yet, lest ye should fail in the exercise, which requireth a figure of this description to be looked upon, I send for your indulgence such a picture as I have been able to procure, setting forth the figure of an omnivoyant, and this I call the icon of God.
>
> (de Cusa, 1928, p. 3)

For de Cusa the, to us, banal phenomenon of depicted eyes that appear to be looking at whoever is looking at them was an iconic device for arriving at an understanding of God's vision. As God is omnivoyant, seeing all instantaneously, his *viso* – glance, gaze, regard – viewing the past, future, present, the near, the distant, as one, in the same timeless moment, so the portrait's depicted eyes 'see' in a way that transcends human vision. De Cusa instructs the monks to hang the painting on a north wall and perceive its wonders, first of static omnivoyance – any looker, wherever he is, feels himself to be the object of its gaze – and then dynamically:

> If now, while fixing his eye on the icon, he walk from west to east, in like manner it will not leave him. Then will he marvel how, being motionless, it moveth, nor will his imagination be able to conceive that it should also move in like manner with one going in a contrary direction to himself.
>
> (de Cusa, 1928, pp. 4–5)

And so on, until the monks, by repeated contemplation of His icon, come to know the mystery of God's omnivoyance and 'the gaze that never quitteth' (p. 5).

The iconic mode of signifying whereby like is signified by like, where the material of an iconic sign, its signifier, is supposed to image or resemble what it signifies, dominates the code of pre-perspectival visual images: just as its arithmetical version – the repetition of signifiers to signify repetition as in two lots of X being XX, three lots of X being XXX and so on – dominates the pre-Hindu Roman code of numerals. It relies upon a 'natural' order of similitude, a world of intrinsic likenesses that exist before signs. Thus, in categorising his gift as an icon, de Cusa appeals to this world of pre-existing 'natural' sight in which it makes sense for the omnivoyance of the depicted eyes to mimic the gaze of God. And thus, too, the use of gold in medieval paintings to signify the presence of God: gold as intrinsically beautiful, changeless, precious, immutable serves as the perfect icon of a God who is beautiful, changeless and so on.

In short, where medieval painted images make God's invisible prior world manifest through 'natural' icons, Renaissance images represent an anterior visual world through a convention of signs, artificially produced by a humanly imposed system of perspective. Interestingly, as the art historian Gombrich (1963, p. 17) points out, Alberti, in his treatise on painting, urged the rejection of gold in favour of white as the appropriate sign for holiness. White, by being at the same time a possible colour on a par with any other colour and a meta-colour, a sign indicating the absence of colour, reflects the systematic ambiguity of the vanishing point. Thus what Alberti wanted white to perform for God's presence in the domain of colour, the vanishing point had already accomplished for the presence of the artist in space.

This rejection of gold – concrete, iconically precious, 'natural', intrinsically valuable – in favour of abstract, semiotically neutral white finds a reflection, as we shall now see, in the signs of money, where the possession of palpable gold is displaced by the intangible assurance on a promissory note.

IMAGINARY MONEY

If most contemporaries found money a 'difficult cabbala to understand', this type of money [assignable bills of exchange], money that was not money at all, and this interplay of money and mere writing to a point where the two became confused, seemed not only complicated but diabolical.

(Braudel, 1974, p. 358)

'Zero stroke' or 'cipher stroke' is the name created by German physicians for a prevalent nervous malady brought about by the present fantastic currency figures. Scores of cases of the 'stroke' are reported among men and women of all classes, who have been prostrated by their efforts to figure in thousands of millions. Many of these persons apparently are normal, except for a desire to write endless rows of ciphers.

(Quoted by Galbraith, 1975, p. 157)

The transition from Roman Hindu numerals based on zero, and from the code of iconic art to perspectival art based on the vanishing point, is reflected in the field of economic activity by a fundamental shift in the structure of money signs that occurred in the passage from feudalism to mercantile capitalism.

In the classical Marxian formulation economic modes of society differ in the manner in which they extract and dispose of the time spent by men in labour surplus to that necessary to reproduce themselves as economic beings in society: in feudalism such surplus value in the form of products became part of the visible wealth of the Feudal lord. The use-value that arose from labour was materialised in products which were concrete and meaningful to the producer, satisfied human needs in a local sense, and were inextricable from the social context of their making. In capitalism, what arose from labour was exchange-value materialised in commodities; these were abstract, lacking in social history, and meaningful only to the extent that they were bought and sold within transactions. For the capitalist, surplus value was turned into invisible capital, and had 'all the charms' as Marx, interested in just such a facility, put it 'of a creation out of nothing'.

To isolate a purely semiotic dimension of the transformation from feudal use-values to capitalist exchange-values, and identify the meta-sign through which the shift from a product to a commodity takes place, we must focus on the underlying system of signs which facilitated these changes – that of money.

The reintroduction of gold money into Europe in the late middle ages superimposed on the prevailing barter economy a universal pricing system. Gold became both the standard against which the value of goods could be measured and the substitute in the mechanism of exchange replacing the exchange of goods by the transfer of currency. There is, however, nothing intrinsically capitalist in the sort of metallic economy brought about by gold; the transactions it made possible were essentially transposed acts of barter. The money which facilitated them lay outside these transactions: money could be bought and sold – a crucial distinction. (True, there existed money changers who might at first glance be considered to have performed such a function; but though they dealt in currencies, they did so only to the extent of exchanging them one for another, bartering them in a manner identical to the bartering of goods for which the currencies themselves had been introduced as substitutes.) The advent of gold money, then, allowed the barter system to replicate itself at another, money based, level. It did not in itself produce any rupture within the medieval barter economy: only when this money could be bought and sold – when money entered into a relation with itself and became a commodity – did the feudal code constructed on the notion of a product become disrupted and replaced by the code of commodities engendered by mercantile capitalism.

But in order to buy and sell money, rather than merely trade one currency against another, a new type of money is needed to provide the medium of exchange and institute the code in which such transactions of currency are to take place. This new money, which will not itself be a currency in the old sense, will introduce itself as a new type of sign; a sign external to and in principle unrepresentable within the sign practices governing the use of gold money. How did such money signs originate?

As a sign, gold money's principal characteristic and mode of operation is iconic, in the sense that the manner in which it signifies derives not from any arbitrary conventional pairing of sign vehicle and signified value, but from gold's physical nature as precious metal, possessing worth and being valuable, prior to any act of signification. As Foucault (1973) puts it:

> The value of [gold] money must be determined by the quantity of metal it contains; that is, it returns to what it was before, when princes had not yet stamped their effigy or seal upon pieces of metal . . . arbitrary signs were not accorded the value of real marks; money was a fair measure because it signified nothing more than its power to standardize wealth on the basis of its own material reality as wealth.
>
> (Foucault, 1973, p. 169)

This reliance on its own materiality, whereby gold money operates through signifiers whose weight is supposed to guarantee the sign values in question, contains an inherent instability. As a circulating sign, gold money runs up against the problem faced in principle by any iconic sign, that of physical debasement. A gap arises between 'good' money (the pure unsullied issue of the state) and 'bad' money (the worn and fraudulently diminished coins in circulation). This gap in signified value between the ideal, nominal signifier corresponding to the face value and the materially debased signifier which reduces the sign to a function of its actual, that is contingent, weight became known as the *agio*. As a kind of average debasement the *agio* was, according to Adam Smith:

The supposed difference between the good standard money of the state, and the clipt, worn, and diminished currency poured into the country from all the neighbouring states.

(Smith, 1976, pp. 474–80)

It was on the basis of this difference between good and bad money that a new type of monetary transaction and a new form of money emerged in those mercantile states, such as Venice and Amsterdam, whose international trade was especially vulnerable to the instabilities caused by debasement. The solution adopted (the same in each state) was for a bank of the state to create a new 'imaginary' coin, such as *Marc Banco, Florin de Banque* and so on, whose value was specified externally, in a global sense, as a fixed weight of gold or silver and internally, in a local sense (via the *agio*) as a determinate but variable amount of gold money exchangeable for it. These imaginary coins were a form of credit issued by the bank. And naturally enough:

This credit was called *bank-money*, which, as it represented money exactly according to the standard of the mint, was always the same real value, and intrinsically worth more than current money.

(Smith, 1976, p. 480)

Such imaginary money was not embodied: it had no physical currency; it did not materially circulate as gold or silver coin; it could not, therefore, be debased. It functioned as a money sign, not through any iconic replication of value in its own vehicle, but by convention, through a mutual understanding between a bank and an individual. In effect, it was a promise to pay, given by the bank to a particular merchant in exchange for gold money.

The individualising of money signs in this way, whereby imaginary money is deictically rooted in the signature of a particular named payee, creates what is essentially a monetary pronoun completely parallel to the visual pronoun generated by the vanishing point. Clearly, this deixis (which, as we shall see later, is the site of the next change in money signs) represents a complete break from the unrooted, freely circulating anonymity of gold coins.

Indeed, in relation to the signs of gold money, imaginary money is, like zero and the vanishing point, a certain sort of meta-sign which both participates in and initiates a new sign practice: bank money, by systematically attaching a sign to current money different from its manifest value, converts gold money into a commodity. It thus has a dual relation to the system of monetary exchange, being both internal to the system as money able to buy goods and be exchanged for appropriate amounts of currency, and external to it – originating the very medium of exchange which allows money to become a commodity.

This dualism between sign and meta-sign is the semiotic reading of the opposition between what was felt to be real and what was imaginary about money signs. The *Mark Banco* or *Florin de Banque* appear as 'real' money, that is actual elements within the total system of money signs, freely exchangeable, substitutable, and on a par with the other signs there. They also appear as 'imaginary' money, that is a meta-sign whose meaning arises outside these signs in a relation of origination to them: since it is only through bank money that gold money moves from a sign iconically determining value for feudal products to a sign among signs in the code of commodities created by mercantile capitalism.

2

Emergence of a Meta-Subject

Each of the transformations described so far, in arithmetical signs, picture signs, and money signs can be thought of as a different model of the following abstract scheme:

There is a *system* (Hindu decimal place notation, principles of linear perspective, mechanism of capitalist exchange) which provides a means of producing infinitely many *signs* (numerals, pictures, transactions). These signs *re-present* (name, depict, price) items in what is taken to be a *prior reality* (numbers, visual scenes, goods) for an active human *subject* (one-who-counts, one-who-sees, one-who-buys-and-sells). The system allows the subject to enact a *thought-experiment* (calculating, viewing, dealing) about this reality through the agency of a *meta-sign* (zero, vanishing point, imaginary money) which initiates the system and affects a *change of codes* (gestural/graphic, iconic/perspectival, product/commodity).

I want now to deconstruct this scheme. What lies at its centre, explicit in the talk of 'prior' reality, is some supposed movement into signification, some shift from object to sign, from presentation to representation, from a primary given existence to a secondary manufactured description. In each of the cases of number, vision, and money a field of entities is assumed to exist anterior to the process of assignation performed by the system. What are taken to be pre-existing numbers are given names, scenes from some supposedly pre-existing visible world are depicted, goods conceived as existing independently of, and prior to, the agency of money are assigned a price. In each case this process of assignation hinges on the meta-sign which both initiates the signifying system and participates within it as a constituent sign. And it is this double ambiguous role played by zero, by the vanishing point, by imaginary money, which ultimately destabilises the scheme presented here and deconstructs the anteriority to signs this reality is supposed to enjoy.

In other words, the simple picture of an independent reality of objects providing a pre-existing field of referents for signs conceived after them, in a naming, pointing, ostending, or referring relation to them, cannot be sustained. What gives this picture credence is a certain highly convincing illusion. Once the system is accepted, on the basis of a perfectly plausible original fiction, as a mechanism for representing some actuality, it will

27

continue to claim this role however far removed its signs are from this putative reality; so that, for example, numerals can be written which name 'numbers' that are unrealisable by any conceivable process of human counting or enumeration, pictures can be painted that depict purely imaginary, non-existent, or visually impossible 'scenes', transactions can be drawn up that price humanly unachievable relations between 'goods'.

The result is a reversal of the original movement from object to sign. The signs of the system become creative and autonomous. The things that are ultimately 'real', that is numbers, visual scenes, and goods, are precisely what the system allows to be presented as such. The system becomes both the source of reality, it articulates what is real, and provides the means of 'describing' this reality as if it were some domain external and prior to itself; as if, that is, there were a timeless, 'objective' difference, a transcendental opposition, between presentation and representation.

From one direction this deconstruction of the anteriority of object to sign can be construed, as we shall see, as the path by which the meta-sign engenders a secondary formation of itself. Each of the signs zero, vanishing point, imaginary money, will now be shown to have, in relation to the whole original system of signs, a natural closure which emerges as a new, highly potent meta-sign, important in its own right, in the codes of number, vision and money. A meta-sign whose action, at one remove from the original 'anterior' field of entities, accompanies a radically different, self-conscious form of subjectivity which I call the *meta-subject*.

CLOSURE OF ZERO: ALGEBRAIC VARIABLE

At the end of the sixteenth century the Dutch mathematician Stevin advocating in his treatise, *The Dime* (Stevin, 1958) the extension of the Hindu system of numeration from finite to infinite decimals, expressed great wonderment at the creative power of zero, at the ability it gave the principle of place notation to manufacture an infinity of number signs.

Stevin rejected the classical notion of number, *arithmos*, as a fundamental misunderstanding of the nature of numbers. For both Plato and Aristotle *arithmos* always, as Klein (1968) in his investigation *Greek Mathematical Thought and the Origins of Algebra* expresses it, 'indicates a definite number of definite things. It proclaims that there are precisely so and so many of these things'. And though they differed on a crucial point of interpretation, 'Plato speaks of numbers which have "visible and tangible bodies" . . . so that in counting dogs, horses, and sheep these processes yield dog-, horse-, and sheep-numbers' (Klein, 1968, pp. 46–7), while Aristotle, concerned to clarify what it means to say that two numbers were equal, saw them as abstractions from particular concrete collections. Both would have assented to the formula 'number as an assemblage of "units" '.

For Stevin the source of error here is not so much the formula itself but the quasi-geometrical interpretation of a 'unit' contained in the classical view that underlies it, the notion that units were abstracted, individualised 'things' that were not (obviously) pluralities and not in fact numbers at all. On the contrary, Stevin argued, the unit was a number like any other; it was not the unit that was the *arche* of number, but the nought. Zero was the proper origin of number, 'The true and natural beginning' (Steven, 1958, p. 499); and just as the point in geometry generates the line, so zero, which he wanted to call *poinct de nombre* gives rise to numbers.

To make zero the origin of number is to claim for all numbers, including the unit, the status of free, unreferenced signs. Not signs *of something*, not *arithmoi*, certainly not real collections, and not abstractions of 'units' considered somehow as external and prior to numbers, but signs produced by and within arithmetical notation. In the language of Saussure's distinction Stevin rejected numbers as signs conceived in terms of positive content, as names for 'things' supposedly prior to the process of signification, in favour of signs understood structurally, as having meaning only in relation to other signs within the sign system of mathematics. In effect, Stevin was insisting on a semiotic account of number, on an account which transferred zero's lack of referentiality, its lack of 'positive content', to *all* numbers. In so doing he overturned the belief in the anteriority of 'things' to signs that that classical formulation of *arithmoi* depends on.

Stevin's primary interest, however, was not semiotic but mathematical. He proposed to extend the principles of the Hindu place notation from the whole numbers to all possible real magnitudes. This meant the creation of a system of infinitely long signifiers which relied for their interpretation on infinite summation, that is, on the process of an infinity of numbers being added together. Thus, just as 333 means $3(1) + 3(10) + 3(100)$, so $0.333 \ldots$ *ad infinitum* means $3(1) + 3(/10) + 3(1/100) + 3(1/1000) + \ldots$ *ad infinitum*. Such non-finite addition requires an infinite limiting process; a phenomenon visualisable in geometric terms as an asymptotic approach of a line to a curve. Stevin's extension of Hindu numerals to an infinite format, which resulted in a numeralisation of the real one-dimensional continuum, had far-reaching consequences for seventeenth century, and indeed for all subsequent, mathematics. Semiotically, it is the *language*, algebra, in which these consequences were developed, and the opposition such language offers between determinate, possibly unknown, but fixed numbers (constants) and the indeterminate non-numerical entities (variables), that is of primary interest.

Algebra, the art of manipulating formal mathematical expressions such as equations, formulas, inequalities, and identities, is co-extensive with the idea of a *variable*. In any algebraic expression, such as for example the identity $(x - y)(x + y) = x^2 - y^2$, the letters x and y are said to be variables, by which is meant that they denote arbitrary individual numbers in the sense that any particular number may be substituted for x and y. A variable is thus a sign whose meaning within an algebraic expression lies in certain other, necessarily absent, signs. In relation to these other signs, which constitute its 'range', a variable is a meta-sign, that is one which indicates the virtual – the potential, possible, but not actual – presence of any one of the particular signs within its range.

The essential mathematical idea of a variable, that is as an indeterminate that can be calculated with as if it were a determinate number, is due to Stevin's French contemporary, Vieta. Unlike Stevin, Vieta did not challenge the classical picture of number. His notion of variable which he called *species* was, therefore, formulated, as Klein observes, in referentialist terms:

> The concept of species is for Vieta, its universality notwithstanding, irrevocably dependent on the concept of *arithmos*. He *preserves the character of the 'arithmos' as a 'number of . . . ' in a peculiarly transformed manner.* While every *arithmos* intends *immediately the things or units themselves* whose number it happens to be, his letter sign intends *directly the general character of being a number* which belongs to every possible number, that is to say, it intends 'number in general' immediately, but the things or units which are at hand in each number only mediately. In the language of the schools: the letter sign designates the intentional object of a 'second intention' (intentio secunda), namely of a concept which itself directly intends another *concept* and not a *being*.
>
> (Klein, 1968, p. 174)

For practical mathematical purposes Vieta's referentialism (repeated, as we shall see, in contemporary accounts) is of no importance. It is only significant, when one asks the question what a number sign is and what it means semiotically for a variable to range over numbers. For such questions, the referentialism behind explanations of indeterminateness in terms of scholastic distinctions between first and second intentions, essentially the opposition between things and signs of things, *is* the point at issue: for it is precisely this opposition that mathematical indeterminacy, semiotically perceived, requires to be unmasked.

The point is central. I shall elaborate it by taking issue with the current orthodox, that is realist, explanation of a variable; a simple, purely syntactical definition within set theory which runs as follows: to say 'x is a variable ranging over the numbers N' means simply that 'x denotes an arbitrary member of the set N of numbers', where to denote a number means to point to the set constituting it. According to the set-theoretical realism behind this definition, numbers – and indeed *all* mathematical entities such as points, lines, invariants, geometrical figures, ratios, constructions, functions, spaces, predicates, relations, and so on – are 'things' called sets. So that mathematical discourse is entirely descriptive and referential: its signs are names, more or less explicit, more or less contained within other names, of determinate set-theoretical objects, its assertions are propositions, unambiguously 'true' or 'false' statements about some prior, extra-linguistic, universe of sets.

What, then, are *sets* as conceived by set theory? They are ensembles, collections, classes and aggregates, of members which are themselves ensembles, collections, classes and aggregates of members: where the regression of membership is imagined to end either in some arbitrarily introduced atomic entities – ur-elements – or, as is actually the case in current practice, in the set-theoretical first cause, the equivalent of zero for collections, namely the empty set ϕ. In this conception sets have precise, unambiguous criteria for membership governed by axioms; they are static, unchanging, determinate things. Theorems proved 'true' about them remain true, and so must always have been true; they are in no sense invented but discovered as timeless objects that simply exist in the Platonic (Parmenidean, in fact) universe of pure motionless being. Sets are in short the 'things', the ultimate *Dinge*, required by a nineteenth century realism immersed in the anteriority of things to signs (of things).

Conceived as sets in this way, the objects of mathematics are subjectless, unauthored referents that exist independently of human agency. By excising the subject from its conception of mathematical activity such realism offers an epistemology as well as an ontology that is semiotically incoherent: it misrepresents proof, for example, as validation of eternal truths about 'things', and misdescribes a variable as a place-holder for the members of some infinite set of such things. As *signs* variables are those which can be replaced by any sign of a given kind. In the paradigm case, that of number variables, the 'given kind' are the number signs, and since these cannot be specified except through the process of counting, it follows that a semiotic characterisation of a variable can only be given in terms of the active, constructing, counting subject. Or to make the comparison in historical terms, the algebraic variable, semiotically perceived, amounts to a re-description of Vieta's *species*: one which reinstitutes the subject – the one-who-counts – into Vieta's discussion, replacing the *arithmoi* there by the purely semiotic picture of number that Stevin so marvelled at.

What is the connection between zero and a variable as meta-signs? Zero functions dually: it moves between its internal role as a number among numbers and its external role as a meta-sign initiating the activity of the counting subject. So it is with the algebraic variable, except that the internal/external duality is enacted at one remove from the one-who-counts. Perceived internally, variables present their familiar appearance as manipulable algebraic objects, as signs among signs within formulas. In expressions like $x + 1 = y, 2x + 3y - z = 0$, and so on, the letter signs enter into full arithmetical relations with number signs: multiplying them, being added to them, being numerically compared to them, being substituted for them, and generally being treated as if they *were* number signs according to a common syntax. Perceived externally, this unitary syntax comes apart, since variables are not of course number signs; on the contrary, they are signs which meta-linguistically indicate the possible, but not actual, presence of number signs.

This duality is mediated by a new mathematical subject, the *algebraic subject*, whose relation to the one-who-counts mirrors the relation between a variable and a number. Thus, the algebraic subject has the capacity to signify the absence of the counting subject, the displacement of the one-who-counts from an actual to a virtual presence. Now at certain points, when variables are instantiated by numbers, this displacement ceases to operate – the two subjects coalesce. So that, for example, the algebraic subject who reads the identity $x^2 - 1 = (x - 1)(x + 1)$ becomes the subject who checks the result of writing, say, $x = 10$; who, in other words, computes – ultimately by counting – the arithmetical validity of $100 - 1 = 9 \times 11$. But this sort of arithmetical localisation is extraneous to the difference between the two subjects: when variables are manipulated as *algebraic* objects within formal calculations any such fusion between the counting and algebraic subject is precluded; and the algebraic subject performing these calculations remains as an autonomous, arithmetically self-conscious, agent whose meta-linguistic distance from the one-who-counts is the source of the difference, when they are considered as mathematical discourses, between algebra and elementary arithmetic.

The semiotic connection between zero and the variable thus emerges as one of symbolic completion: by ranging over *all* number signs, that is over all possible records that can be left by the subject whose sole capacity is to repeat, the algebraic subject performs an operation of closure on the infinite proliferation of number signs that come into being with zero. In effect, the algebraic number variable is a sign for the signs that can, at least in principle, be produced by the one-who-counts.

CLOSURE OF THE VANISHING POINT: PUNCTUM

In his *Vision and Painting: The Logic of the Gaze* Bryson (1983) draws a fundamental distinction between two stages of perspectival painting in terms of the requirements of physicality, of spatial locatedness, that the system imposes on the spectator:

> What we are really observing, in this first geological age of perspective, the epoch of the vanishing point, is the transformation of subject into object: like the camera, the painting of perspective clears away the diffuse, non-localised nebula of imaginary definitions and substitutes a definition from the outside. In its final form . . . the only position for the viewing subject proposed and assumed by the image will be that of the

Gaze, a transcendent point of vision that has discarded the body . . . and exists only as a disembodied *punctum*.

(Bryson, 1983, p. 107)

In terms of the semiotic activeness charted so far, this transition from what Bryson calls the 'Glance to the Gaze', from the vanishing point to the punctum, from a corporeal spectator, objectified by the deictic insistence of the 'pure' perspectival image, to one who is disembodied, who views the painting from an unoccupiable, purely notational, point in space, will correspond to a shift in subjectivity: from the subject created by one meta-sign to the subject of a secondary meta-sign which forms the semiotic closure of, what it renders as the previous, system of images.

To see how this comes about, how the first epoch of perspective in the fifteenth century gives way to its second culminating form two centuries later, we shall look at two paintings, *The Artist in his Studio* by Vermeer, and *Las Meninas* by Velasquez, each of which, in very different ways, exemplifies the illusion of vanishing point perspective through an image which unmasks it, and denies it in favour of a radically more complex, self-conscious, form of viewing.

If there is a single vanishing point in Vermeer's painting it is certainly not evident. On the one hand, the usual indication (a pair of orthogonals that can be seen to intersect) is evaded: the foreground and background chairs and the artist's stool, all suitably right-angled, are placed obliquely to the frame, the table which appears square to the frame displays only one orthogonal, and so on. On the other hand, the usual indication is curtailed: the flagstone floor, though it implies the conventional continuity between spectator and scene, and in earlier perspective paintings would have given an immediate determination of the vanishing point, is here so flattened, so reduced in scope and deliberately masked by objects, that it determines nothing beyond its declaration 'floor'.

Clearly, then, the viewer is not being asked to enter the painting by focusing on and occupying the central geometric absence created by a vanishing point. Instead, there is a more pressing, visually immediate absence, put there by Vermeer and not as a result of perspectival requirements, marked by the back of the artist's head – that of his face, which positions the spectator. From this absence of vision one is impelled to another, the face of the model, whose downcast if not closed eyes point to the final absence of sight, the white death-mask staring blindly upwards from the table. This chain of absences, at first direct but unseen, then oblique, downward, and masked, and ultimately open but sightless, vividly concretises Vermeer's ghostly and enigmatic celebration of seeing, or rather (though he would perhaps have appreciated the elision) his celebration of the painting of seeing.

Vermeer's title, *Di Schilderkonst*, understandably but incorrectly translated

Illustration 7   Jan Vermeer: *The Artist in His Studio.*

as *The Artist in His Studio*, means the art of painting, and his depiction of an artist (perhaps Vermeer) making a depiction is precisely about the process of picture making itself. As a sign depicting the making of perspectival images, Vermeer's painting embodies a visual meta-sign, a sign about picture signs. And the artist responsible for this meta-sign, the one who has painted the scene, is nowhere to be seen. Not only can he not be traced through any identifiable vanishing point, with the result that the painting is seen in multi-perspective, it can be viewed from an arbitrary position, but he has expunged any trace of his visual presence from the act of painting it. The convex mirror at the base of the chandelier (unlike the mirror in van Eyck's Arnolfini painting two centuries earlier reflecting back van Eyck to the spectator) gives back no image of the painter. On one side it shows the light by which the scene is rendered visible to the internal artist painted by Vermeer, and on the other an indistinct reflection of this same artist; in the middle, instead of the painter, it is the chandelier, prosaically inserting itself, that is reflected (see Illustrations 8 and 9).

Illustration 8 Jan Vermeer: detail of chandelier from *The Artist in His Studio*.

If, as seems reasonable, the seated figure can be taken to depict Vermeer, then, because Vermeer could not have seen himself in this way, his painting represents a scene he has imagined. The scene was nowhere but in his head. But if a scene can be literally nowhere, have no 'real' location, what then is the difference between presenting and representing? The priority of things to signs which sustains the distinction seems to disappear. As if to counter this merging of the literal and the metaphorical, of 'things' and signs (of things), of the real and the depicted, but in fact compounding it, Vermeer emphasises the fiction of the thing/sign opposition by painting the same leaves three times: first as posed or advertised 'reality' on the model's head, then, at the moment of being painted by the figure, as a represented 'sign' of this so-called reality. And then again as, unobtrusively signified back-ground 'reality' within the curtain on the left of the painting. Thus visual perception and the painting of this perception cease to be opposed categories; Vermeer no longer *records* perceptions but, as Bryson (1983, p. 116) puts it, 'notates them, and then demonstrates (paints) the act of notation'.

Illustration 9   Jan van Eyck: detail of mirror from *The Arnolfini Wedding*.

Vermeer's image, then, like all the meta-constructs encountered so far, operates ambiguously between its lingual and meta-lingual roles. Internally, as a sign within the code of perspectived paintings, it is a single image, a picture sign among picture signs, depending on other paintings for the interpretation of its narrative, its structure, the meaning of its constituent signs, and so on. Externally, the meta-sign calls attention to this very system of images and to the account of perception it promotes; and in so doing offers the spectator an unlocated subjectivity, inviting him to occupy the place of the unsituated artist, the absent, invisible, notional subject who painted the image; the one without whom Vermeer's picturing of the act of painting would be merely another depictive painting – one which accepted, rather than put into enigmatic question, the illusion of representation offered by perspectival images.

As the north European algebraic variable is to the zero of the Italian Renaissance, so Vermeer's painting, one of the culminating images of the Northern Renaissance separated by more than two centuries from the 'first geological age of perspective' of Brunelleschi and Alberti, is a continent apart from its Italian forebears. It makes sense to ask, therefore, whether there are semiotic features of Northern, essentially Dutch, painting which might have facilitated the emergence of such a meta-sign.

S. Alpers (1983), in her persuasively illustrated book, *The Art of Describing*, provides an analysis of Dutch seventeenth-century art and the theories of vision inseparable from it, which yields a response to this question. One which starts from the difference between two ways of drawing the transversal and orthogonal grid-lines of perspective: the Italian method of construction, and the distance-point method recommended by Viator in the first North European treatise on perspective at the beginning of the sixteenth century. Her illustrations of the difference, taken from Giacomo Vignola, are shown in Illustrations 10 and 11.

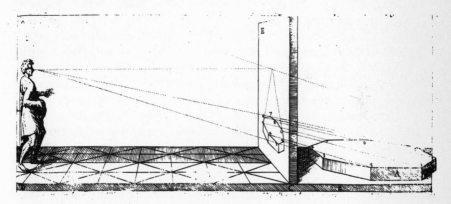

Illustration 10   Giacomo Vignola: the first *'regola'* or the *'construzione legittima'*.

Now it is geometrically obvious and well known that these two rules can be made to yield identical systems of perspective lines; making it easy to appropriate the second, later rule to the first (seeing it, for example, as nothing more than a practical Northern device, a draftsman's rule of thumb, for the swift production of transversals). Such an understanding of distance-point construction would, Alpers argues, violate a fundamental distinction between the two rules. What is significant about Viator's method, at least in

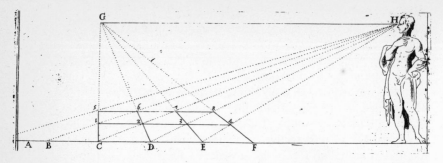

Illustration 11   Giacomo Vignola: the second '*regola*' or distance point method.

relation to Dutch art, is the emphasis it places on the existence of an internal viewer. So that in Saenredam's image, for example:

> The eye of the viewer (which in Alberti's construction is prior and external to the picture plane), and the single, central vanishing point to which it is related in distance and position, have their counterpart here *within* the picture.
>
> (Alpers, 1983, p. 53)

In an argument, too historically textured and ramified to summarise here, Alpers offers the presence of such an internal viewer – a depicted *looker* as she says – as a paradigmatic feature of Northern art, one intimately bound up with the essentially *descriptive* mode of Dutch visualisation with its attachment to the visual representation of knowledge through maps, plans, diagrams, and drawings of the world as seen through the microscope. As Alpers points out, the figure gazing up at the organ in Saenredam's interior is not, as might appear, merely a device of scaling inserted to underline the grandeur of the church's architecture; but, on the contrary, is the organising visual focus, the point of visual entry into Saenredam's image (see Illustration 12). The spectator and the 'looker' fuse. What is emphasised and made available to the viewer is an ocular, ambulatory presence inside the image, and not a view from without determined by external design as required by Italian perspective. Alpers' account makes the uncannily life-like 'realism', the strange hyper-verisimilitude found in so much of Dutch art, a comprehensible effect of this internalisation of the vanishing point. Saenredam's drawings of churches, Vermeer's Delft, and so on, persuade the spectator of their visual immediacy, the physical occupiability of what they depict, precisely because in front of them there is 'no prior view to establish a position . . . from which, as we say, to take in the work' (Alpers, 1983, p. 41).

Alpers' concept of the 'looker' suggests a mediating term between two visual subjects: a subjectivity situated between the perspectival subject,

Illustration 12 Pieter Saenredam: *Interior of the Church of St Bavo in Haarlem,* 1636.

associated with the primary meta-sign of the Italian vanishing point, and the meta-subject associated with its closure, with the punctum found, so far, in Vermeer's painting.

One can thus articulate a sequence of four visual subjects that span the movement from Gothic art to the culmination of Northern painting in Vermeer's *Art of Painting*:

(1) the Gothic subject, the one who uses Roman numerals, whose mode of signifying is dominated by the iconic, made up of what Bryson (1983, p. 116) calls 'diffuse non-localised nebula of imaginary definitions'; (2) the perspectival subject, coded by the vanishing point, situated outside the frame in a relation of imagined identification with the artist's viewpoint, the result of the Gothic subject having been objectified mirror-like into a visual pronoun; (3) the 'looker', the figure of internal vision in Dutch art, an internalisation of the perspectival subject, whose interior presence calls into question, and so suggests the absence of, any exterior point of view; (4) the meta-subject, engendered by the punctum, able to *signify* what the presence of the 'looker' can only raise as an interpretive possibility, namely the necessary absence of any externally situated, perspectival seeing.

Corresponding to these four phases of subjectivity one has four types of signification:

(1) no meta-sign; (2) meta-sign = vanishing point; (3) internalised meta-sign; (4) meta-sign = punctum.

And, in turn, four forms of anteriority – the presumed primacy of 'things' to signs which refer to them:

(1) *Anteriority is non-existent.* Medieval image makers did not categorise their efforts in terms of referentiality. They neither claimed nor denied a posterior relation to some real, waiting to be depicted, physical world. The pictorial values they prized were the mythic, the numinous, the spiritually potent, not those of accuracy or depictive 'truth'; the space of Gothic images was not representational, but conceptual and iconic (recall de Cusa's interest in the portrait of a face in terms of its capacity to iconise God's vision.) (2) *Anteriority is present.* Italian perspective painting was founded on the fiction of a framed portion of nature, a detached fragment of some prior visual 'reality', being represented with truth and accuracy, to the viewer; its image makers prized copying and perfect mimicry. To be praised as an *imitatore della natura* or, more hubristically, a surpasser of nature, was the greatest compliment they sought. (3) *Anteriority is in abeyance.* The visual world does not so much precede the viewer as exist alongside him, coterminous with his viewing presence; the internal 'looker' and the reality he

sees are simultaneously presented artefacts – a phenomenon which leads Alpers to observe, about Saenredam's images, that 'such pictures are not properly architecture viewed, in which an external viewer is presented with a view of architecture, but rather *views of architecture viewed*' (Alpers, 1983, p. 52). (4) *Anteriority is deconstructed. The Art of Painting* renders perspectival viewing, the framed picture as a geometrised simulacrum of a prior world, impossible. There is no unsignified 'real' which can be, accurately or otherwise, simply recorded and depicted. All that is seen is already a pictured universe. The world and visual signs for the world cannot be separated: 'Observation is not distinguished from what is observed. That is the grand illusion that the picture . . . creates' (Alpers, 1983, p. 168)

Despite its manifold differences – in scope, iconography, style, mode of composition, pictorial setting, cultural assumptions – Velasquez' image delivers, and seems intended to deliver, a semiotic lesson cognate to Vermeer's on the illusive difference between presenting and representing (see Illustration 13). Certainly, in terms of content, the two images present a striking set of common features and preoccupations with respect to which they exhibit parallel or polar opposite responses.

Both paintings are signs that contain, as essential elements within their schemes, already signified 'realities', constructed images, designs, depictions – the pattern of leaves reproduced in Vermeer's curtain, his scrupulously wrought map of Holland dominating the background, Velasquez' accumulation of studio canvases, barely discernible through the gloom or the flattening of perspective – which call attention to the paintings' preoccupations with the nature of visual representation, with the illusions attendant on the business of painting signs to stand for things.

Both are paintings of artists painting: one seated, absorbed in the process of seeing, motionless, faceless, private, caught from behind; the other standing, dynamic, frontally and publicly present, interrupting his painting with a look indicating his awareness of being seen.

Both depict an artist painting a portrait of a figure from life, physically present to them as models. In Vermeer's image the representation of the model, a girl who, idealised as the historical muse Clio, is already a representation, is visible to us, the viewers. In Velasquez' painting the model is the Infanta, the royal Margarita, present to us in unidealised form, but her representation is invisible. The opposition between the paintings these doubles of Vermeer and Velasquez are producing reflects this alternation of absence and presence: Vermeer's internal painting looks to be a small and delicate portrayal of his model, open and declarative, against the absent and hidden vision of its producer. Velasquez' internal canvas, enormous and mysterious, mocking through its revealed back the pretensions of pictorial depth, has an image on it as obscured and absent as its producer is defiantly present.

Both paintings feature mirrors that conceal as much as they reflect.

Illustration 13   Diego Velasquez: *Las Meninas*.

Vermeer's, withdrawn from prominence, and naturalised, as if it were there accidently as part of a contingent background, nevertheless calls attention, by a comparison with earlier convex mirrors in Northern painting, to what it fails to reflect, showing only the painter's double and the light he paints by, but no painter. Velasquez' mirror, placed so advertently at the back of his image at its visual centre, likewise shows no painter but reflects, and insists that we notice the fact, two ghostly figures.

It seems to be generally accepted that the figures are the king and queen of Spain in whose service Velasquez' picture is being produced. Any interpretation of *Las Meninas* has, then, to explain their mirrored status within the intentional structure of the painting. Foucault, in an intricate reading of the subjectivities organised within the painting, claims that this mirror, by containing the vanishing point of the entire picture, occupies a pivotal and ambiguous role:

> For in it there occurs an exact superimposition of the model's gaze as it is painted, of the spectator's as he contemplates the painting, and of the painter's as he is composing his picture (not the one represented, but the one in front of us which we are discussing.
>
> (Foucault, 1973, p. 14)

According to this we become aware of the place outside the space of the painting, directly opposite the mirror, from which we, the spectators, organise these subjectivities: the persons reflected in the mirror, for whom the foreground figures have been arranged, are standing where we stand. Velasquez' double is looking at them, at us and at himself; or rather, at the absent Velasquez who has painted this whole scene.

In a recent essay, *Las Meninas and the Mirror of the Prince*, which offers a definitive account of the painting Snyder (1985) dismisses Foucault's reading on the grounds that it is based on a fundamental error: the vanishing point is not, as Foucault (and others) have maintained, within the mirror but is located well to the right of it near the elbow of the figure in the doorway. This being so the mirror cannot contain the reflections of the real, corporeal king and queen standing in the foreground opposite the vanishing point; rather it reflects a 'reflection' of them, an *ideal* of their royalty which Velasquez' whole picture is to be taken as manifesting and celebrating. Snyder's reading which is embedded in a persuasively detailed appreciation of the role played by mirrors, as metaphors for the 'ideal' in seventeenth century Spanish thought, is convincing. Whether it displaces Foucault's quite different interest in the exchange of subjectivities is open to doubt. Certainly Foucault's error about the vanishing point removes the grounds for his reading, but not necessarily the insights that the reading makes available. In fact, the readings are, in the end, as much complimentary as mutually excluding. Where Foucault (1973, p. 16) describes Velasquez' painting as the place where 'representation undertakes to represent itself' and emphasises its organisation around 'an essential void: the necessary dis-appearance of that which is its foundation – of the person it resembles and the person in whose eyes it is only a resemblance', Snyder (1985, p. 564) insists not on means but ends, on the function of the painting to externalise the very idea of the 'ideal', so that '*Las Meninas* is a speculation about speculation, a reflection by an exemplary artist of an ideal image that engenders images'.

From the formal semiotic point of view adopted here, both Velasquez' and Vermeer's paintings can be seen to contain, rest on, and be entered through, an absent subject – the painter/viewer – which the mirror must fail to reveal. The subject we are being asked to confront, through a chain of absences in Vermeer, a void in Foucault's reading of Velasquez, or a non-corporeal 'idealised' reflection in Snyder's reading, is a meta-lingual one, a visual *meta-subject* at once notional, invisible, and absent, who by making evident the false anteriority of visual things to visual signs, allows depiction to become, for the first time, self-conscious. Moreover, like Vermeer's image, *Las Meninas* operates as a sign about signs, a meta-sign whose domain is the mode of depiction itself. Its offer to the spectator, an invitation to occupy the place of the one-who-paints-the-image, is addressed to the meta-subject; a subject who, through the ambiguous action of the painting, sees – through what is after all a perspectively-based image – the limits of perspectived seeing.

This meta-subject within the code of visual signs, who appeared with the variable as the algebraic subject within the signs of mathematics, will appear again, below, in relation to a new form of money sign. Before this I want to give another version of self-consciousness emerging from the activity of a subject depicting himself depicting; one which occurred at the same time as the construction of the algebraic subject by Stevin and Vieta.

Montaigne in the medium of words, written but fundamentally different from the written media of mathematical, visual, or monetary signs, not only saw himself making precisely such a self-depiction in his autobiographical *Essays*, but also, characteristically, perceived the illusion behind it:

In framing this portraits by my self, I have so often beene faine to frizzle and trim me, so that I might the better extract my selfe, that the pattern is thereby confirmed, and in some sort formed . . . . I have no more made my booke than my booke hath made me. A booke consubstantiall to his author: of a peculiar and fit occupation. A member of my life. Not of an occupation strange and forraine, as all other bookes.

(Montaigne, 1889 'Of Giving The Lie')

Where Vermeer and Velasquez painted images of themselves painting, Montaigne wrote himself writing, inscribing an image of himself within the text; an image busily writing ('scribbling' he called it) about the imaginary scenes Montaigne chose to lay before him. When Montaigne affirms that the self he is depicting cannot be separated from the process of depiction, that it is 'in some sort formed' by the very activity of framing its portrait, he is articulating in the written words of his *Essays* what *Las Meninas* and *The Artist in His Studio* render through visual signs: namely, the illusion of anteriority, the fantasy of a world of the 'thing' – in Montaigne's case some unitary, preexistent, waiting to be written, 'true' self – prior to a domain of the 'sign of the thing' which represents it.

What are the imaginary scenes Montaigne puts in front of his double in the text? What, in the *Essays*, corresponds to the object of internal depiction, to the girl-as-Clio Vermeer's double is painting or the royal Infanta being painted in Velasquez' image? Montaigne conceived himself to be a creature in motion, to be identified as a self only through activity, through the pattern of his responses to the world. This being so, Montaigne depicts his double – the one who says 'I' in the *Essays* – as writing down his (the double's) reactions, his responses to this or that circumstances imagined for him, from a place outside the text, by Montaigne.

It is natural to perceive the mirror reflexivity here in terms of painting and to see the *Essays* as giving 'not just a painter painting a picture of himself but a painter painting a picture of himself painting a picture and so on' (Sayce, 1972, p. 73); a metaphor which leads to a self situated at some infinite vanishing point. But the image of painting, unless it is cognisant of the deconstruction of object and sign accomplished for example in the images of Vermeer and Velasquez, rests on precisely the false anteriority they reveal. Another metaphor, non-inscriptional and closer perhaps to Montaigne's sense of himself as a being known only through activity, is that of theatre. For once Montaigne admits that his 'self' is a performance, that what he observes has been posed for the observer, his supposedly autobiographical text cannot but reflect this duplicity: 'his medium, in order to transmit *that* aspect of his self, must reveal not the role that is played but the actor in the process of performing' (Rider, 1973, p. 78).

Such a self-conscious staging of the act of writing about writing makes the *Essays* into a certain kind of meta-theatre in which the actor, having perpetually to divulge the lie of acting, and moving ambiguously between the depicted self who says 'I' and the absent unknowable author, is a textual meta-subject: an agency able to convey, via a written text, the illusion that there exists a self, a prior 'thing', anterior to written depictions of that self.

To say this is in no sense to deny the materiality of the world, to pretend that there is no corporeal presence answering to the historical figure called Montaigne whose 'self' is the subject-matter of the *Essays*, and in relation to which one recognises his text as autobiographical. Rather, when Montaigne (1889, 'The Affection of Fathers') writes that '*Je me suis presente moy-mesme a moy, pour argument et pour subjet*', he must be interpreted as denying the existence of some pristine, pre-textual self, some original and given 'me' (*moy, moy-mesmes*) being referred to by an independent and posterior 'I' (*Je*) in favour of a written construct that precisely transcends the I/me opposition. Thus, the sense in which the *Essays* are autobiographical, that is the nature of the semiotic relation between the meta-subject – the self thus constructed – and the self of the historical 'Montaigne' is not one of description or reference (transparent, abstract, neutral language pointing to a pre-linguistic thing), but a relation between signs that rests on an iconic and motivated resemblance between an embodied and a textual self.

In an exactly parallel way, behind the abstract and unsituated character of the visual punctum lies a material world of sight, perception, and physical apprehension which is not *described* by the images of Vermeer and Velasquez as if it were there independently of these images. The obvious 'life-likeness' of such paintings, their recognisability as visual evocations, testifies to an iconism between signs that offer themselves as seeing (depictions) and the seeing of seeing (meta-signs that depict such embodied depictions).

CLOSURE OF IMAGINARY MONEY: PAPER MONEY

In the sign systems of mathematics and painting, zero and the vanishing point give rise to secondary meta-signs which form their semiotic closures. We shall now witness the same phenomenon occurring within the field of money signs.

We saw how bank money, the imaginary ideal money of the *Marc Banco*, by assigning a price via the *agio* to gold money, produced a certain kind of written credit, a monetary promise made by a bank to a named, individual merchant. And though such a note could be passed from hand to hand, and could, therefore, in some sense circulate freely, its link to the original merchant, no matter how complex the circuit of exchange, was never erased. The secondary meta-sign which forms the closure of imaginary money, arises from the complete severing of this attachment, the separation of money signs from traceable named owners, and the creation of a new, depersonalised and anonymous, form of money sign – that of *paper money*.

This attachment of bank money to particular persons arose from the fact that it, like any promissory note (as well as bill of exchange, receipt, IOU, note of indemnity, cheque, and so on), was an inherently deictic, that is to say, indexical sign. Its meaning as a money sign pointed to and was inseparable from the physical circumstances of its use. One can say that its utterance as a sign was governed by a demonstrative personal pronoun tying it to the concrete particulars of a temporally located, named individual, since in order to circulate as money it needs to be turned over and endorsed, that is written to a payee by its owner through a reference, a date, and a signature. The presence of such a pronoun sharply separates imaginary money from money in currency. Indeed, it was in relation to the signs of currency – the circulating gold coins – that imaginary money appeared as a meta-sign indicating, through this pronoun, a mercantile subject who was not present, and indeed could not be mentioned, within the code of exchange determined by circulating gold money.

The deixis inherent in imaginary money is the monetary analogue of the pronoun of place and point of view particularised by the vanishing point. And, as with the vanishing point, to emerge from it and form its closure, to become de-deictified, depersonalised, freed from the attachment to a spatially particularised viewer or owner, imaginary money has to be replaced by a different sort of sign presentation; a presentation that makes a new type of monetary promise – the kind of promise, for example, printed on English and Scottish bank notes (see Illustrations 14 and 15).

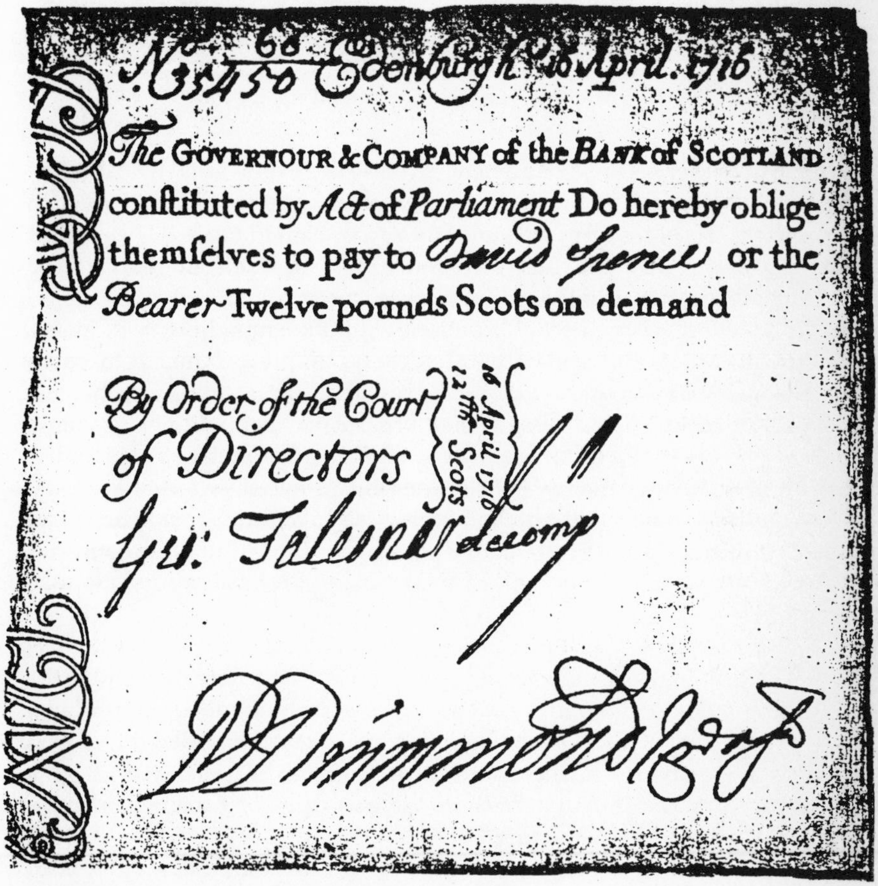

Illustration 14   Scottish twelve pound note, 1716.

At the end of the seventeenth century the Bank of England introduced, and the Bank of Scotland popularised, the printed bank note. The notes illustrated here display two versions of the promissory formula. In the

Illustration 15   English one pound note, 1955.

Scottish note there is the older deictic promise to an individual whose name has been written in, together with an alternative general promise (which in fact renders the older form redundant) to an unnamed bearer. The English note dispenses with the first pronominalised, indexed alternative, and simply addresses its printed declaration to 'the bearer'.

The move from a deictic promise, with its embodiment in dates, individual names, and apparatus of witness, to one promising to pay a de-personalised anonymous *bearer* is highly significant; and it was achieved, in terms of historical process, against a particular semiotically revealing form of legal resistance concerning the signing of monetary notes within English Law. Neither the resistance (nor what it reveals) would have been evident if bank notes, with this same promise to an unnamed bearer, had been first introduced in Scotland or France, since the law of these countries required no written discharge of a monetary promise made out to a 'bearer':

> Unlike [in] England, the right at common law to pass notes payable to the bearer on demand without assignation or endorsement had never been questioned; the Scots Law being like that of France founded directly on the Roman Code, which permitted any Creditor to transfer or assign a debt without the Debtor's sanction, the transferee or Assignee having a right to sue in his own name.
>
> (Graham, 1911, p. 5)

The legal point at issue was whether the common law of England (for which a 'contract' was always between named individuals) should be interpreted as allowing 'things-in-action' (which included bills of exchange as well as promissory notes) to be assignable to strangers. Whether or not, in other words, the practice of 'making bills (payable to bearer) transferable without a slow and expensive assignation, or even any endorsement' should be permitted. No final judgement was ever given. Initially the practice was allowed for bills of exchange but disallowed for promissory notes; a judgement which was then overturned to include promissory notes. This inclusion was then almost immediately reversed with the decision that 'all writs being promissory notes and not bills, were illegal, and could not be assigned or transferred; and finally this last judgement was ignored, and notes payable to a 'bearer', requiring no endorsement or validating signature, enjoyed a free *de facto* circulation.

The oscillation in law here between signing and not signing a note, between a named and an unnamed individual, between a particularised payee and generalised unlocated bearer, was the reaction of a judiciary reluctant to abandon the familiar localised subject addressed by a deictic promise – the subject of a contract – for the global, anonymous subject indicated on paper money by 'The Bearer'. The bearer is a *variable* subject, a subject in meta-lingual relation to any particular named and dated individual (the temporary owner of the note at a particular time) able to instantiate it, a meta-subject inscribed in the meta-sign 'paper money', whose analogue, in the signs of mathematics, is the algebraic subject.

Zero and the vanishing point gave rise to their closures through the process of a certain deconstruction. The illusion of anteriority, that is the belief that numbers and visual scenes were prior to the arithmetical signs that named or the signs of painting that depicted them, was exposed by the construction of meta-signs that insisted on 'things' and signs-for-things being coexistent. These were meta-signs, moreover, for which the categorial opposition between anteriority and posteriority was dissolved – it being as 'true' to hold that numbers and scenes were posterior, creations of the very system of signs invoked in order to name them, as to believe the opposite.

For money signs the illusion of anteriority collapses at exactly the point when the printed bank note is recognised as an instrument for *creating* money. Unlike metallic money:

[Paper money] soon involved the artificial manufacture of money, of ersatz money, or if you like a manipulated and 'manipulable' money. All those English bank promoters and finally the Scot John Law gradually realised 'the economic possibilities of this discovery, whereby money – and capital in the monetary sense of the word – were capable of being manufactured or created at will'.

(Braudel, 1974, p. 362)

The scandal of paper-created money, that is money written or printed into existence, was well appreciated by those who lost their 'real' money to Law's

financial wizardry. And it has haunted the users of paper money and all the
financial instruments descended from it ever since. The scandal is the loss of
anteriority: paper money, instead of being a representation of some prior
wealth, of some anterior pre-existing quantity of real gold or silver specie
becomes the creator, guarantor and sole evidence for this wealth (see Illustration 16). And yet paper money still offered to the bearer of a note, the
exchange: palpable specie, money in the hand, for an anonymous paper sign
that can go and come from anywhere (the Chinese called it 'flying money'),
thereby insisting on the existence of anterior wealth waiting to be
redeemed. The scandal is that of self-creation:paper money, as a circulating
money sign, appeals to the very anteriority that as a creative meta-sign it has
the capacity to deconstruct.

Illustration 16   US dollar bill silver certificate, 1957. A silver certificate which unlike
the standard dollar bill explicitly promises redemption in specie.

Unsurprisingly, paper money was viewed with hostile suspicion –
exchanging real gold or silver for a flying paper note seemed lunatic – and
enthusiastic greed – the bank note's ability to create wealth seemed
unlimited. In the United States, where the widespread use of paper money
was pioneered, these responses crystallised into a debate in the early
nineteenth century between rival monetary philosophies.

Marc Shell (1980) sees in this 'debate about coined money and paper
money [which] dominated American political discourse from 1825 to 1845',
a wider, far-reaching conflict about the nature of signs – aesthetic and
literary as well as monetary – about the nature, that is, of the difference
between 'reality' (things) and 'appearance' (signs-of-things). Certainly, the
issue between the 'gold bugs' (for whom money meant gold, paper money
being merely a licensed fraud) and the 'paper money men' (whose notes
promised absent specie stored in a bank) was that of monetary reality and
appearance (see Illustrations 17 and 18). And as with the vacillation of the
English judiciary over signing or not signing a promissory note, the conflict
arose from the refusal to surrender a palpable reality to an invisible

appearance which the new paper sign required of its users. For the 'gold bugs' money was solid, physical and real, a precious commodity which was owned by individuals, a 'thing' as opposed to a sign; and they refused the offer made by the 'paper money men' to become 'bearers' – anonymous globalised versions of themselves – of notes that were mere insubstantial signs for money.

Shell, who is interested in the effect of this conflict on aesthetic representation, shows how Poe, in his story 'The Gold Bug', creates images that display the suspicious, uncertain, mysterious, fraudulent, and ghostly nature of the promise of gold on a piece of paper.

A SHADOW IS NOT A SUBSTANCE.

Illustration 17 'A shadow is not a substance', 1870. Specie reality and 'greenback' appearance.

In the cartoon 'A Shadow is not a Substance' for example, the specie can be viewed as one cause of the shadow. The specie and the sun are two links in the chain of cause and effect which a detective might say

Illustration 18   Milk tickets for babies. 'In Place of Milk', 1870.

produces the shadow. In 'The Gold Bug' the events in the plot and the eventual discovery of gold are not connected by this kind of necessity. To say that the design of the gold bug on the paper is a link in a chain of symbols or events which leads inevitably to the gold is, adopting the terms of the caricature, to say that the shadow is the cause of the substance rather that vice versa. According to the Gold Bugs, this is the ostensibly absurd position of the Paper Money Men, of whom Legrand seems to be one as he marches through the dark forest with the designed paper clutched in his hand.

(Shell, 1980, p. 21)

Shell illuminates Poe's story as a detective fiction whose mystery – unravelled through a melodrama of subliminal clues, cyphers, invisible writing, hidden treasure – is paper money's scandalous capacity to create gold. In the story, Poe makes the written instructions to the buried treasure (his narrative proxy for the promissory formula of the bank note) appear unnaturally, out of nowhere, as letters cryptically emerging from a blank sheet. He plays with and mocks paper money's ambiguous duality, its ability to appeal to the anterior existence of gold at the same time as it deconstructs, via its capacity to *manufacture* money, the very possibility of this anteriority. Ultimately in the story symbols – the signs-for-things – and 'things' co-exist and create each other.

Later we shall see that in the end, within the present-day world monetary order, paper money's promise of payment, its promise to deliver some absent gold or silver, goes by default: on presenting a dollar bill to the US Treasury or a pound note to the Bank of England for redemption, the bearer would not be given any specie but would simply be offered a copy of the note being redeemed. Within such a tautological model of exchange, paper money becomes flying money that can never land (see Illustration 19).

Illustration 19   German billion mark note, 1923. Hyper-inflated paper money.

NATURALISING META-SIGNS INTO SIGNS

The movement from the primary meta-signs of zero, vanishing point, and imaginary money through a characteristic deconstruction to their closures produces a new signifying capacity which, in each case, assumes the priority of objects to signs in order to deny it; a semiosis in which signs are seen to create the very objects they are taken to be depicting, naming, and representing.

And if the source of this denial, the meta-subject who exposes the illusion that objects are anterior to signs, appears in its different manifestations within mathematical, visual, textual, and monetary signs as a variable, invisible, unsituated, anonymous and absent agency, then the meta-sign which constitutes the means through which it operates requires a certain obliteration: namely, the nullification as a *meta*-sign of the original and primary sign whose closure it is.

There is a moment in each of the codes that I have discussed when the fact that this change has happened becomes visible, when the meta-sign in question appears in an already naturalised form as a mere sign: when zero is accepted as just a number among numbers, its meta-lingual role at the origin of these numbers forgotten; when the vanishing point is absorbed into the painting as a location among others depicted there, its geometric initiation of the painting's design ignored; and when imaginary money is internalised as just more money, its meta-lingual distance from gold money suppressed.

What is forgotten, ignored, suppressed – in fact repressed – here is the original subject, or rather, the *agency* of this subject, the activity of the one responsible for originating, through the primary meta-sign, the entire system of signs. And it is in the place left empty by the primary subject that the meta-subject occurs. Its relation to the absented subject being that of temporary fictional identification, as when the subject of algebra imagines himself to be the one who makes the material marks of counting, the visual meta-subject sees himself embodied and situated in the place of the artist's double, the bearer of a paper note believes himself to be the individual, deictically present 'owner' of specie.

This move which naturalises meta-sign to sign in the codes of mathematics, vision, texts, and money, can be mapped onto a familiar and banal phenomenon in the code of spoken language, namely the literalisation of figures of speech, the death of metaphors, metonyms and the like. However, the question: what, literally, is a dead metaphor and how and at what point do metaphors die? seems problematic and unanswerable. For Nietzsche, for example, whose attack on 'truth' initiated the sense of the difficulty lying behind any simple interpretation of 'literal', it was a question of forgetting:

> Truths are illusions whose illusionary nature has been forgotten, metaphors that have been used up and have lost their imprint and that now operate as mere metal, no longer as coins.
>
> (Nietzsche, quoted in Culler, 1981, p. 203)

If we attempt to avoid the circularity of Nietzche's use of metaphor (a monetary one at that) to locate the metaphorical death of metaphor, and speak from within a purely formal semiotics, we can say merely that semiotically a particular meta-sign is alive, its figurative and meta-lingual content still vital, as long as the primary subject, for whom the distinction between literal and figurative is itself still alive and uproblematic, is not, in the ways we have seen, forgotten, ignored, or suppressed; as long, that is, as the meta-subject, for whom presentations and representations coincide, has not yet made an explicit appearance within the code in question. In other words, the literality which sustains a metaphor is put into question at some point in the passage from a fully present primary subject to the signified absence of that subject. For Western depictive painting such a point is almost visible: between the presence of the perspectival subject (unquestioned acceptance of perspectival literalism) and the explicit denial of the possibility of this literalism in the meta-paintings of Vermeer and Velasquez there occurs, as we saw, the internal depicted figure of the *looker*. By offering an internalised image of the perspectival subject such a figure neither embraces such a subject nor takes any part in signifying its absence; rather the figure is a sign which stands in the code at a place between the two: by challenging, on the one hand, the idea of literality, of a clear-cut distinction between prior reality and a subsequent figurative depiction of that reality, without on the other hand, in any way suggesting how such an idea might be denied or shown to be illusory.

It is a commonplace to describe the sorts of sign transformations that have occupied us as part of a general increase in conceptual abstraction that occurred with and through the emergence of Renaissance science. Certainly, algebra is a more abstract, less concrete, art than arithmetic, written calculations are more abstract than abacus manipulations, paper money is more abstract than imaginary money, the use of gold money is a more abstract activity than exchange by barter, and so on. But this sort of simple linear ascent through levels of abstraction, though adequate perhaps for certain purely internal histories of codes, conceals the agent responsible for these changes, the subjectivity in relation to which (and only so) they can be made intelligible. In the codes of mathematics, vision, text, and money, it is the active constructing subject who, by taking part in a thought experiment, makes an abstraction; an experiment in which the subject is enabled to occupy a new semiotic space, one which relies essentially on a reference to the absence of signs that were previously – before the experiment – conceived in terms of a positive, always present, content.

Of the signs I have talked about those of mathematics are generally held to be the most abstract. On the view presented here – that abstraction as an attribute of signs is essentially the result of a subject absenting himself – such is not the case. Zero is neither more nor less abstract than the vanishing point or imaginary money; all arise from and indeed facilitate the same sort of self-absenting move.

But zero is, as we observed earlier, a more universal and conceptually naked sign for absence, whose connection to the idea of 'nothing' creates an altogether more primitive and elemental source of abstraction. And it is this coupling between zero and the paradoxical idea of 'nothing' that will occupy us next.

3

Nothing: Zero

Nothing is
But what is not
(Shakespeare, *Macbeth*)

THE ICONOGRAPHY OF '0'

The thesis advanced so far runs as follows. In each of the written codes of mathematics, painting, finance a fundamental shift occurs with the introduction into that code of a particular meta-sign for the absence of certain signs. Each meta-sign – zero, the vanishing point, imaginary money – disrupts the code in question by becoming the origin of a new, radically different mode of sign production; one whose novelty is reflected in the emergence of a semiotic subject able to *signify* absence. Further, these meta-signs beget others, they engender closures of themselves, secondary meta-signs whose meaning lies in their capacity to articulate a central, and previously implicit, feature of the meta-signs which gave rise to them: namely that the opposition between anterior 'things' and posterior 'signs' (for things) is an illusion, a fiction of representation unsustainable when faced with the inherently non-referential status of a sign for the absence of signs.

These deconstructive movements – zero/variable, vanishing point/ punctum, imaginary/paper-money – from originals to closures declare themselves as a loss of anteriority: a declaration made possible by the emergence of a new self-conscious subject, the meta-subject, able to *explicitly signify* this loss in the discourses of number, vision, and money.

To the written codes of mathematics, painting, finance, and the autobiographical text already discussed, one could add other examples; the written code of Western musical notation for instance. In this the cognate of zero would be the sign for a silence, the meta-note designating the absence of other notes – a blank, a rest – introduced into musical notation in the late medieval period. And the closure of this meta-sign, the musical homomorph of the algebraic variable, would then be the emergence of the well-tempered scale which initiated tonal music in the seventeenth century. But instead of pursuing yet another elaboration of a by now clearly discernable semiotic phenomenon, I want to return to the meaning of the sign 'nothing', in particular the connection between 'nothing' and zero.

The concept of nothing – the void, emptiness, that which has no being, the non-existent, that which is not – is a rich and immediate source of paradoxical thought: the sign 'nothing' either indicates something outside itself and thereby attributes the condition of existence to that which has none, or the sign has no referent, it does not ostend, it points to nowhere, it indicates and means no more than what it says – nothing. Paradoxical formulations such as this admit, as we shall see, many different responses. They can be interpreted as mere rhetorical games, word play, idle poetic mirrors, ultimately empty of meaning; or as modes of irony, sites of ambiguity that allow forms of nihilism to be simultaneously accepted and, because of the dangers of heresy, repudiated; or as meta-logical arguments against the referent, against the notion that signs refer to something prior to and outside themselves; or as vehicles of ascetic practice or mystical speculation, iconic tropes which constitute a mimicry in words, of God's mysterious – absent – presence.

In her encomium, *Paradoxia Epidemica*, of paradoxes and the paradoxical mode in Western intellectual and rhetorical discourse, Colie (1966) gives much thought to 'nothing', tracing a path from pre-Socratic debates about the void, through Christian theological disputes concerning the attributes of God and the dialectical opposite to 'nothing' – All, the Cosmos, Infinity – that impinge on questions of individual existence, survival, oblivion, and annihilation, to the *nihil* rhetorical paradoxes of the sixteenth century, the struggle to formulate the concept of a vacuum in seventeenth-century science, and the visual oxymorons for 'nothing' constructed in Dutch still-life painting.

Colie's principal interest in 'nothing', impacted in an almost overwhelming density of historical detail, is its metaphysical fecundity, its endless capacity to generate paradoxical thought. By contrast, the present account is interested in the purely semiotic fecundity of the mathematical sign zero, its ability to serve as an origin, not of paradox, but of sign creation. In some obvious but obscure sense nothing and zero are connected; and, in a narrow formal sense, can be made to look identical. Zero signifying an absence of signs and 'nothing' signifying an absence of things seem to occupy the same space once one denies the illusion that 'things' are anterior to signs. But zero and 'nothing' are manifestly separate, moving in different historical and linguistic terrains, and being carried by very different signifiers: against words – 'nothing', 'rien', 'nihil', and so on – zero, represented by the symbol '0', has a physical shape, a graphic presence independent of particular languages, with its own iconography.

But what can be learned from its iconography? Is not the shape of zero accidental? A mere historical contingency? What, in any case, has its material or geometrical manifestation to do with the *idea* of nothing?

Consider the mathematical, purely notational problem that zero addresses. It arises as a gap, an empty region, within the place notation for individual numerals signifying, in the decimal case, the absence of 1,2, . . .,9. An iconic, mimetic approach to the writing of this absence – taken for example by Babylonian mathematicians for nearly two millenia – might be the use of an empty space to signify it; so that, for instance

11, 1 1, 1 1, 1   1

would notate eleven, one hundred and one, one thousand and one and ten thousand and one respectively. But the scheme has an obvious defect: the right-hand space merges with the blank surface of writing, making 11 ambiguous between eleven, one hundred and ten, eleven hundred, and so on. Moreover, and for the same reason, an empty space is not transportable: unlike the other numerals it cannot be reproduced, written independently of its syntactical presentation within particular numerals, without it merging with the space used to separate words from each other. Signifying absence by absence is not, then, a stable and coherently interesting option for writing down zero.

On the contrary, one signifies absence by making a (graphic) presence, by writing something down, inscribing an unambiguous, permanent, transportable mark. What sort of mark is suitable to inscribe absence?

There is the minimalist possibility of the pure monotone, the atomic mark: the single irreducible dot, point, stroke. But this carries the meaning of presence and nothing else, since the writing of a dot – an undifferentiated, atomic, ur-mark, a monad – has to mean at the least 'there is a sign here'. To mean more, to be able to signify something other than the declaration of its own signifying presence, would require a mark to have a physical attribute, a graphic characteristic, *other* than that of being a signifying mark. Now there is of course nothing to prevent this ur-sign of presence from signifying *by convention* an absence, and so, in the context of numbers, from being used as a symbol for zero. But though such a usage can be found in early occurrences of the place notation it was not, at least in the Western tradition, the historically preferred solution.

Moreover, there is no pressing need to force the ur-sign of presence into a *conventionally* written representation of absence: the iconic approach of the Babylonians can indirectly be retrieved. Instead of literal mimesis, copying a space by a space, one can *depict* an absence through a signifier that contains a gap, a space, an absence in its shape. The most elemental solution, the ur-mark of absence, is any instance of an iconographic hole; any simple enclosure, ring, circle, ovoid, loop, and the like, which surrounds an absence and divides space into an inside and an outside. Thus, presumably, the universal recognition of 'o', 'O', '0' as symbols of zero. And thus a circle of associations linking zero and 'nothing'. As Colie observes (1966, p. 226) 'from the 'O' to the egg was an obvious step since the egg was the symbol of generation and creation; since, too, it bore the shape of zero, contradictions of all and nothing could be constructed on eggs'; which one can continue through the mystical O of the Kabbalah, the Hollow Crown which served as an icon of *ex nihilo* creation; the great circle of white light signifying infinity for Traherne; the origin and place of birth – 'nothing' as slang for vagina in Elizabethan English; to the icon of de-creation and self-annihilation in the shape of the circle made by a snake swallowing its own tail.

But iconography goes on its own peculiar paths: graphically based metaphors and metonyms for absence and nothing are an inherently limited source of insight. The particular written shape of a signifier and the range of its graphic and kinetic associations seems in the end a capricious and somewhat arbitrary route to its meaning. The signifier for zero, for example, could be other than the symbol '0', and was: later Babylonian mathematicians used a double cuneiform wedge, and the Mayans a figure resembling a half open eye, and so on. The connections, or lack of them, between 'nothing' and zero, if they are to go beyond fortuities of shape, must be located in Western intellectual discourse; within the discussions, arguments, and modes of thought, Greek, Jewish, Christian, which attempted to give, or refuse, a significance to 'nothing'.

GREEK–CHRISTIAN NOTHING

Orthodox Christianity in Western Europe from St Augustine's moral foundations to the scholastic legacy of St Aquinas took its conception of God as a being knowable or unknowable to man, from Greek theology and metaphysics and its image of God as a maker, the Creator of the world, from Jewish monotheism. In so doing it saddled itself at the outset with a fundamental contradiction, a logical dilemma which it never resolved, about the ontological and eschatological status it was to assign to 'nothing'. Christianity thus inherited two mutually incompatible accounts of the first, original, initiating act of creation. For the Greeks this was the moment whereby God gave form to primitive matter which was itself eternal and uncreated; the world was an artifice of God, God was its architect, not its maker. Against this the God of the Old Testament created the whole universe – its matter, substance, form, design – out of nothing.

Moreover, this insistence that 'something' was always there, that there was never 'nothing', which separates Greek artifice from Hebrew *ex nihilo* creation, is the passive expression of a direct and agonistically fraught confrontation with 'nothing' that runs deep inside Greek philosophical discourse: the metaphysical and theological discussions within which Plato and Aristotle cognised their God are hostile to the very idea of the *void*. This hostility – ultimately a refusal to countenance that emptiness, nothingess, that which is not, was a 'thing' that could be signified – permeated all of

Greek thought, with the notable exception of Epicurean atomism to which we return below, from the Eleatic precursors of Socrates onwards.

The Greek refusal of the void was at once a philosophical proposition, a conclusion explicitly and safely debated within the domain of rational discourse. Ontologically it was impossible to attribute being to 'nothing' since 'nothing' is that which *is* not, and epistemologically 'nothing' was without meaning. It could only be known by knowing nothing (a paradox which, as we shall see, Socrates made much ironic play with in relation to his own knowledge). At the same time there was a phobic and terrified reaction by Greek thinkers to emptiness, a shrinking back from the disruption, chaos and anarchy that they feared would issue from granting signification and presence to that which is not. Both the fear and the reasoned argument inseparable from it have their original expression in the picture of an eternal changeless universe given by Parmenides.

Parmenides, like Plato and the Christian theologians after him, separated the universe into the world of appearance, the gross physical habitation of the senses, always in motion, heterogeneous and fragmented, and the world of reality, the world of pure form, God, unchanging Being, which was full, homogeneous, indivisible, timeless and One. To give assent and credence to such a bifurcation it is necessary to be convinced, at least it was so for Greek thinkers, by rational argument. One had to be logically persuaded that change and plurality, however much they *seem* real to us, must be illusions, mere dream-like phenomena of appearances which seem to *be* but in truth are not and can never be part of Being. Parmenides, and more famously his disciple Zeno, gave many arguments defending his unitary static cosmos. Those that survive are principally in the form of paradoxes which forced their interlocutors into accepting that the ideas of motion and plurality were inherently contradictory and incoherent and were therefore, by a *reductio ad absurdum* argument, not real.

Zeno's celebrated paradoxes (in which a stadium was impossible to traverse, arrows could never arrive at their targets, Achilles could never overtake the tortoise, and a moving body must always fail to pass another body) had a profound effect on the structure of Greek thought – on its mathematics no less than its theology and cosmology – far beyond their original focus of defending the Parmenidean 'one' from the pluralism of Pythagorean number mysticism with its belief in a Being forever being enlarged from the unreality of the void. Certainly, there is no record of the conclusions argued for by Zeno having been refuted, or any indication that the paradoxes were the subject of disabling criticism, or could be explained away. In particular, Aristotle's description and supposed dismissal of them more than a century after their appearance is cursory, opaque and lacking in appreciation of their dialectical subtlety.

If, for the moment, we focus on mathematics, then it is plausible to hold, on the evidence of Euclid's elements alone that, far from ignoring them, Greek mathematicians were shocked by the Eleatic arguments into a certain kind of silence, an unarticulated mistrust and suspicion of the ideas of motion and of plurality; especially any explicit mention of these ideas within what was supposed to be a valid mathematical argument or legitimate mathematical definition. Thus, in the case of motion, for example, they rejected as invalid a well-known and easily achieved solution to the famous problem of trisecting an angle by ruler and compasses because it rested on a reference to a moving point as an essential part of its argument. Again, in terms of definition, they denied any role to motion. All objects of Greek mathematical thought such as numbers, ratios, points, figures, and so on, were characterised as wholly static fixed entities so that, for example, the figure of a circle was defined as the locus of points equidistant from some given point and not as the path of a moving point. If the paradoxes of motion, then, encouraged a mathematics conformable with Parmenides' static changeless reality, what of his attack on plurality?

For plurality one must read the dialectical opposition which Parmenides extracted from it; namely, that which is limitlesss, without end, infinite, against that which is nothing, has no being, the void. A typical formulation of Zeno runs:

> If there is a plurality, things will be both great and small; so small as to be infinite in size, so small as to have no size at all. If what is had no size, it would not even be . . . If there is a plurality, things must be just as many as they are, no more and no less. And if they are just as many as they are, they must be limited. If there is a plurality, the things that are are infinite; for there will always be other things between the things that are, and yet others between those others. And so the things that are are infinite.
>
> (Zeno, quoted in Kirk and Rower, 1957, p. 288)

What the Zeno-Parmenides interdiction of motion, the void, and infinity engendered within Greek mathematics was a hypostasised literalism and an attachment to visually concrete icons which influenced mathematics from the time of Euclid to the Renaissance (and beyond: a version of Parmenidean stasis is central to the dominant present-day conception of mathematics in which mathematicians are supposed to apprehend eternal truths about entities – 'structures' – in an unchanging, timeless, static, extra-human world, Rotman (in press)). Thus, in cognising mathematical entities in visuo-spatial terms as physically palpable icons, so that for example the number x meant an ideal length x units long, Greek mathematics interpreted x^2 as the area of a square, x^3 as the volume of a cube, and only with great difficulty could give any meaning to x^4, x^5, and so on. Within this form of iconised cognition negative numbers, algebraic abstraction as opposed to geometrical construal and zero as a sign marking an *absence* are impossible to conceive. The idea of infinity either as a completed process or a limitless extension (tainted by the disruptive contradictions of Zeno's arguments but seemingly essential to mathematical cognition) became the source of an uneasy fear witnessed, for example, in Euclid's mistrust and ambivalence to the axiom of parallels with its implicit reference to an infinitely prolonged length.

If the idea of 'nothing', through the opposition void/infinite, was a source of anxiety and unease in mathematics, and if more generally, it was in logic and rhetoric, as Colie (1966, p. 222) puts it,

> technically dangerous, wild, at the loose edge of conceptualisation and of discourse, nullifying – literally – ideas of order and ordination, . . . psychologically destructive, threatening the familiar boundaries of human experience,

then in the psychologically more vulnerable and fraught regions of ontology and theology it inspired a form of terror. For Aristotle, engaged in classifying, ordering and analysing the world into its irreducible and final categories, objects, causes and attributes, the prospect of an unclassifiable emptiness, an attributeless hole in the natural fabric of being, isolated from cause and effect and detached from what was palpable to the senses, must have presented itself as a dangerous sickness, a God-denying madness that left him with an ineradicable *horror vacui*.

In short, the Greek reaction to the void, characterised by unease, fear, and horror, was one of psychological denial. Within the full indivisible universe of Being there could be no fissure, absence, hole, or vacuum; the void did not exist, it could have no being, it was not.

Confronted by the need of the Christian church to accept the Genesis account of creation *ex nihilo* such a denial was no longer sustainable, and Christian theology was forced to recognise 'nothing' as something; a thing which had a presence, an originating but somehow unreal, part in the scheme of things-which-are, and as something which had to be given a sense, equally unreal, in relation to a God who acted upon it in order to create the world.

St Augustine, though he absorbed the God of Parmenides and Plato and their abhorrence of the void through the neo-Platonist writings of Plotinus and not from Aristotle, assigned an eschatological status to 'nothing' – it was the devil – which neatly Christianises the sort of horrific object Aristotle was at such pains to deny. For St Augustine 'nothing' was a kind of ultimate privation, the final and limiting term of that which was absent, lacking, lost, which had been subtracted and taken away from the original presence and fullness of God. To be in state of sin was to enclose within one's spiritual being an absence of God. Conversely, to be in a state of grace was to be filled with God's presence. Within this dialectic of spiritual absence and presence where goodness was God, and evil – the inevitable fruit of sin – the arena of

His absence, 'nothing' is equated with the ultimate evil: the non-being of 'nothing' becomes the being of evil – whose physical incarnation is precisely the devil.

There is in this privative solution to 'nothing' a difficulty that borders on blasphemy, since it would seem that *before* the creation out of nothing there was something missing, lacking, something not yet part of God's being which was to be subsequently supplied by the creation. St Augustine's answer, elaborated ingeniously in his theory of time, was that in creating the world God also created time itself, and so God, being outside of time, could never have lacked what he always had. The issue however – that is essentially what could and could not be ascribed to God, the nature and status of God's attributes – remained a dangerous one within Christian theology. Any attempt to refer too positively or too directly to God's relation to 'nothing' could be easily converted into heresy and unbelief. Hence St Aquinas' ruling, for example, that God could only be described and spoken about in a mediated way through negative affirmation. God was not finite, not specifiable, not mortal, not changeable, not temporal, and so on. Within this Aristotelian-based negativism God, loving everything abhors nothing, and indeed destroys and nullifies 'nothing' in order to create the world.

But this attempt to negate the problem of 'nothing', by a formulaic transfer of Aristotle' horror of the void onto God's transformative overcoming of it, was more an avoidance of the void than any real engagement with a sign signifying no thing. Not only was the destructive impact of *ex nihilo nihil fut* not to be contained, as we shall see when we encounter that which comes from nothing in *King Lear*, but, for two centuries before Shakespeare's play, the double image of 'nothing' and 'everything' was in itself too interestingly subversive and enticing – in rhetoric and mathematics and logic as well as theology – to be kept under doctrinal restraint. Perhaps if zero had not made its appearance within Christian Europe, much of this larger interest in 'nothing' would not have occurred, and 'nothing' might have stayed within the writings of Aquinas and the Schoolmen as a remote theological issue. But this was not the case, and if from the tenth to the thirteenth century the church's hositlity to 'nothing' was successful in confining zero to Arab mathematics, and so staving off the threat of nullity it presented, the neo-Aristotelian apparatus of concepts inherited by Christian theology was too fixated against absence to even impinge on the larger issue of zero as a sign. Confronted with the rising surge of attention focused on *nihil* in mathematics, rhetoric, and literature engendered by the impact of zero, Christian theology ignored the source and attacked the nihilistic consequences, the heretical and atheistic dangers of believing in and talking about 'nothing'.

As one would expect, it was mathematics that saw the first attempt to incorporate infinity and nothing into its range of signifieds. Already among the later scholastics in the fourteenth century there is a growing interest in infinity and infinite processes. Indeed, the use of infinite addition – combining infinitely many number signs together – to form finite numbers (as in $1 + 1/2 + 1/4 + \ldots + (\frac{1}{2})^n + \ldots = 2$) or infinite numbers (as in Oresme's demonstration that the sum $1 + 1/2 + 1/3 + \ldots + 1/n + \ldots$ exceeds any finite magnitude) initiated the theory of infinite series which was to give a mathematical escape from Zeno's paradoxes. A century later, the writings of Nicholas de Cusa, a vigilantly orthodox theologian and certainly no heretic, were openly full of the possibilities of the infinitely large and infinitesimally small.

Such fascination with the infinite *omnis* and the vacuous *nihil* that went with it was safe from heresy so long as it was confined to the spiritually neutral domain of mathematical signs; the church could hardly mount an inquisition against all the secular users of Hindu numerals. But if the *nihils* of mathematics were secure from the taint of atheism those of rhetoric and the nihilism they bordered on were another matter.

Colie (1966), in her survey of the *nihil* poems and the *nihil* paradoxes of the fifteenth and sixteenth centuries, points to the mimicry of the divine inherent in such forms as the source of their danger:

> In the Renaissance one can find many such paradoxes, appealing because of their impossible affirmations and opportunities of double negation. All affirmations about 'nothing', it turned out, might be taken as analogues to God's original act of Creation, bringing 'something' out of 'nothing' . . . *nihil* paradoxes aspire to the imitation of God's unique act. In precisely that imitation lay the danger: paradoxes about *omnis*, or all . . . might be regarded as pious imitations of God's plenist Creation, but *nihil* paradoxes were another matter altogether. They were engaged in an operation at once imitative and blasphemous, at once sacred and profane, since the formal paradox . . . parodied at the same time as it imitated the divine act of Creation. And yet, who can accuse the paradoxist of blasphemy, really? Since his subject *is* nothing, he cannot be said to be impious in taking the Creator's prerogative as his own – for nothing, as all men know, can come of nothing. Nor indeed is he directing men to dangerous speculation, since at the very most he beguiles them into – nothing.
>
> (Colie, 1966, p. 224)

Thus, such beguilements, avoiding blasphemy and the dangers of heresy through disowning what they seem to avow, allow their authors to sport with 'nothing' by playing the fool. And indeed, the *nihil* paradoxes and rhetorical conceits about 'nothing' that burgeoned in the sixteenth century were part of a literature of Folly, an *amphitheatrum sapientiae socraticae jokoseriae* of wise Fools and Doctors of Ignorance that has its origin in Socrates' ironic disavowal of knowledge, runs through de Cusa's celebration of foolishness and Erasmus' *Praise of Folly*, and is ultimately turned in on itself and deconstructed by Montaigne in his *Essays*.

Socrates, in declaring 'all that I know is merely that I know nothing' was ironically allowing 'nothing' to puncture a certain ideal of self-knowledge in which one knows 'all'. His declaration does not, of course, mean what it says. For, to know nothing is to know no thing and in particular not to know the thing which *is* your knowing nothing, and so on. The paradox plays on the simultaneous difference and identity between two I's: he who knows and he who is known. And it forces an oscillation between subject and object which it does not, cannot, resolve. It creates, in other words, a fissure, a hole in the full indivisible knowing 'I' at precisely the point where such an 'I' has to cognise 'nothing' in relation to itself. And it goes no further..

In terms of our earlier discussion of signs Socrates paradox, though it disrupts an existing sign – the familiar subjective I of discourse – initiates no new sign, no meta-sign pointing to the absence of signs at the site of the disruption. Like all paradoxes, and that is the point of them, Socrates' conundrum is self-contained, it cannot transcend the puzzle it establishes: it points to nothing outside itself other than the dissolution of its own terms. Unlike Montaigne's confrontation with the delphic injunction to 'know thyself' which creates a meta-sign for a new self-conscious subject, Socrates' irony has no meta-lingual dimension to it. Nor is this surprising if we understand that Socrates, in playing the Fool, was very specifically playing the Greek Fool: one who, however much he ironised about knowing nothing, was not, because of his prior and unquestioned denial of the void, able to know 'nothing'. In denying emptiness the iconic literalism of Greek thought had necessarily to deny any rational presence to that which is absent. Socrates, while forcing us to recognise that the knowing 'I' cannot be always unfracturedly present, had no means to *signify* – by signs which would necessarily have to refer to the absence of signs – this lack of presence. Thus by nullifying the capacity to know, reducing knowledge to nothing, Socrates' paradox achieves a certain sort of epistemological self-annihilation: the 'I' of discourse, as a sign for a full indivisible unitary self who knows, is ironised out of existence.

If Socrates impaled that which as a philosopher he professed to love – the act of knowing – on nothing, then St Jerome (Illustration 20) strove to annihilate the act of living within the world, to negate and retreat from that world of mundane sensual everyday reality he had loved. In so doing he legitimised, and became the sanctified model of, the tradition of Christian ascetic self-abnegation and annihilation in the face of the infinitude of God.

Abjuring the world, excising one's presence from it, is not to destroy it or destroy the self (Jerome and his monastic followers did not of course advocate suicide) but to swear permanent absence from it, to nullify being in the world, and see it for what it truly was: an arena of sin, lust, and empty vanity. To achieve this world-negating vision one had to follow the path of

Illustration 20 Albrecht Dürer: *St Jerome in His Study.*

ascetic withdrawal, the familiar *via negativa* of opposition, self-denial, renunciation and retreat. One had to absent the love of friends, physical pleasures, spiritual ease and sexual desire through the dialectical negatives of hermetic isolation, fasting, scourging the self and abstinence.

The process of ascetic self-annihilation has to come to an end. When all else is gone God is still present: when the whole world has been renounced sentient physical presence must remain. But physical presence is temporary, a moment in oblivion to be reclaimed at any time by death. And to forget this, to be beguiled by life and be blind to its utter impermanence was not to have escaped the world but be trapped in the vanity of being. Hence the necessity for *momento mori*, those metonymic signs of the passage of time and of universal decay, like hour-glasses and skulls, which serve as prophylactics against vanity, reminders of death, annihilation and the ephemerality of the world.

In Dürer's depiction the saint huddles over the bible, his existence given over to pious contemplation, reading, studying and translating the word of God. When he turns from God's word to the world he confronts an hourglass reminder of the swiftness of life's passing. When he looks up he sees first a crucifix, an icon of God's death in the world, then, again juxtaposed against the outside world, a skull, an icon of Man's death, and then the lion lying with the lamb, an icon of Paradise: the end and promised reward of physical being. All has been reduced and stripped to a bare and stark duality: God/presence of death, eternal heaven/transient world, infinity/abyss of nothing.

Unlike for the paradoxist, who is forced to equivocate his relation to 'nothing', the heretical dangers of consorting with 'nothing' are obviated for the ascetic precisely because he places it at the centre of his repudiation of the world. To see the world in terms of 'nothing' – vanity and emptiness – becomes the point of that long and arduous route through negation to the final union with God. But the ascetic desire for nothingness is safe from heresy only so long as it adheres to the authority of God's moral law. Whatever else in the world he repudiates the ascetic must remain attached to the moral *presence* of God, to the obligations upon his will and therefore his actions in the world that this presence imposes. Hence the necessity for St Jerome to obey the injunction, in this world, to translate God's word so that men might be saved. To negate this, to claim that Faith alone, without the subjugation of the self that issues from obedience to moral law, was sufficient for salvation was to press the impulse to nothingness into a state of outright heresy.

In the seventeenth century such an heretically extreme form of nihilism known as Quietism, practised by Miguel de Molinos and his followers, was persecuted by the Jesuits. Molinos was a Spanish priest who

> developed his extreme Quietist outlook and practice in Rome and died in an Inquisition prison; his impulse to supress the will to the point where God took over and worked His own way led him to accept any sexual temptation or aberration as the work of the Devil upon a passive, and therefore sinless, believer, who was thereby intensified in his quiet

repose in God; at his trial he admitted to his antinomianism . . . and, as was natural in a Quietist, in the end offered no defense.
(Unamuno, note by the editors Kerrigan and Nozick, 1972, pp. 442–3)

Molinos' moral anarchism, reversing Jerome's sexualisation of Man's love of God into a belief that sexual union was ultimately a form of divine love, was itself enough to have aroused the Inquisition against him. But beyond this was his attempt to annihilate his will, his desire for *nada*, his longing for self-annihilation, for the embrace of 'nothing' as a form of being: his wish to become and to *be* nothing – for that, within the terms that the inquisition imposed on the nature of 'being', was the sin of spiritual self-destruction.

If the Christian ascetic courted heretical nihilism by pursuing a divine union of self with God beyond the constraints of moral obedience in the world, then Christian mysticism, from Meister Eckhart onwards, by seeking total *oneness* with God represented, for orthodox theology, the extreme nihilistic heresy of divine usurpation, a hubristic assumption by the mystic of the original nothingness of God himself. In his account of Eckhart in *Religion and Nothingness* Nishitani observes how the difference between union and oneness with God issues from the distinction Eckhart made between God as *a* being – the Creator, Love, the Divine Presence, and so on – and God as the godhead, conceived as nothing other than the underlying *ground of being* of God, his 'essence' that transcends all particular modes of actuality that can be imagined of His being and becoming. For Eckhart it was necessary to go beyond a union, a personal joining with a soul on one side and God conceived either as a subject or an object on the other, to an identification with the 'absolute nothingness' that constitutes the godhead itself. In this identity there is no longer any meaning in the separateness of a personal soul and God: 'As God breaks through me, so I, in turn, break through him' (Eckhart, quoted in Nishitani, 1982, p. 63). For Nishitani, interested in placing Eckhart within a tradition that contains Heidegger's writings on Nothing, Eckhart's importance and originality is to be found in his finding of the godhead in the absolute nothingness that lies beyond the 'personal God who stands over against created beings' (Nishitani, 1982, p. 62), a location where, in the nothingness before He created the world *ex nihilo*, He had already uttered *I am that I am*. We shall encounter this terminal/originating nothingness again in what is perhaps Eckhart's source, the *Zohar* Kabbalah of Moses de Leon.

One can say that from whatever direction, whether it be the source of heretical nihilism in Eckhart, the incarnation of evil for St Augustine, the site of terminal self-deprivation for St Jerome, the object of Aristotelean horror for St Aquinas, the vehicle of moral suicide for the Jesuits, responses to 'nothing' within the discourse of orthodox European Christianity charac-terised it as the locus of what was irredeemably negative and evil; a place where the presence of God was constantly in danger of being emptied out, denied, nullified, repudiated through apostasy, heresy and unbelief; a place of void to be religiously 'a-voided.'

Unsurprisingly, then, the Christian need to graft Hebrew *ex nihilo* creation onto a Greek theogeny filled with *horror vacui* was the source of a certain unease from which orthodox rationality had to psychologically defend itself. It did so either by exercising a form of repressive denial which met what it saw as the destructive potential of 'nothing' by doctrinally surrounding it with silence; or by involving itself in a form of splitting: a falling back into gnosticism that produced an irreconcilable opposition, the Good world in conflict with the Bad world, God's All counterpointed to the Devil's Nothing.

Moreover, in precisely the same way that Socrates' Nothing, by being the agent of an absence in the previously full and indivisible knowing self, marked the place of an epistemological disruption, so 'nothing' allowed within Christian discourse – and this was its heretical danger – the means of a parallel theogenic disruption by introducing the possibility of an *absence of God*, a falling short from God's total unfractured omni-presence. And, as with Socrates' nullification, the disruptive hole within God's unitary being caused by 'nothing' was semiotically barren: it did not issue in a meta-sign through which this absence could have been signified, recognised and discursively elaborated.

All this prompts an obvious question. Given that Christian thought inherited the problem of 'nothing' through its need to accept the Hebrew account of creation in Genesis how did *Jewish* theology, unburdened by Greek denials and horrors of the void and forced from its inception to make its own sense of creation *ex nihilo*, cognise 'nothing'? The question needs elaborating and I shall return to it below. Before doing so, I want to fill a hole left in the earlier discussion of Greek thought concerning the void.

Abhorrence of emptiness, though a central element in the thinking of Parmenides, Zeno, Socrates, Plato, and Aristotle, was not universal within Greek thought. The atomists (Epicurus, Leucippus, but principally Democritus) accepted the existence of the void as a rational, coherent concept. The universe in all its manifestations was not, as Parmenides insisted, a plenum – full, indivisible, motionless, and one – but was composed of a plurality of atoms in movement which, though themselves were indivisible and so on, had come together in the void to form the physically real, material, empirical world. Democritus' materialism, permitting reference to 'nothing' and antagonistic to explanations of reality in terms of a God-inspired Purpose or Final Cause postulated by Aristotle, was as a result double anathemised and suppressed by Christian theology as both heretical and atheistic.

It was only late in the Renaissance, when emptiness became a pressing object of materialist investigation, that a recrudescence of Democritean Atomism occurred. In the seventeenth century, two fundamentally new 'nothings' fought for existence against the Aristotelian *horror vacui* and the inevitable Jesuit charge of atheism that defended it: the 'nothing' of a physical vacuum – a hole in the all pervading life-giving plenum of air – theorised by Pascal and others as a real, physically present something; and the 'nothing' of empty space – a place devoid of materiality – with respect to which Newton could distinguish relative from absolute motion.

The historical relevance, importance and intellectual support provided by Democritus' materialism to the establishment of these 'nothings', what Colie calls (1966, p. 221) 'that underground stream [which] turned out to be the sacred river feeding the new physics', seems widely accepted. As indeed is the close connection between such 'nothings' and the mathematical insights and preoccupations of their proponents:

> Blaise Pascal was eminently suited to such experimentation on so paradoxical a subject as *le vide*. His scientific and mathematical interests ran to the paradoxical, the improbable, and the ambiguous: his work on infinitesimals and infinite series and on permutations and combinations led to his remarkable contributions . . . to probability theory. He was concerned . . . with the kind of unsolved problem which is fundamentally irrational, and denies altogether the formulation of conceptual limits. His interest in the vacuum is of a piece with his attraction to such problems as those of infinite series and probability theory. He knew that the vacuum was by definition an 'impossible' subject, that the establishment of its actual existence implied not only a revolution in physical thought but a revolution in moral and ontological thought as well.
>
> (Colie, 1966, p. 254)

There is, however, from the standpoint of the present essay, something methodologically unsatisfactory, some misplaced adherence to a model of historical 'influence' and causation, behind such a description. Talk of Pascal's psychological predisposition to be interested in the problem of emptiness and of 'sacred' historical rivers sustaining it ignores the semiotic matrix within which such interest, interpreted in terms of the signs which were to encode such physical 'nothings', could not but occur. Pascal, Torricelli, Newton and other did not, after all, exist in a semiotic void with regard to 'nothing'. They had at their disposal, and were in fact immersed in, the whole practice and mode of discourse about 'nothing' built into the Hindu numeral system. Colie's account of Pascal, which is much alive to his mathematical interests, particularly his fascination with infinity, makes no mention of zero. In a sense this is perfectly understandable: unlike the question of infinity, zero was not problematic for Pascal. It was not, in fact, an explicit item of mathematical concern for him. But, as will be obvious by now, the mathematical infinite was the fruit of the mathematical nothing: it is only by virtue of zero that infinity comes to be signifiable in mathematics.

Now Pascal, psychologically driven as he no doubt was to contemplete emptiness, silence, nothing, a vacuum, was nevertheless not unfamiliar with the mathematics of his day. He knew Stevin's work celebrating the decimal notation and had read Vieta's work on algebra. He thus had, to aid his contemplations of *le vide*, two highly articulated meta-signs based on the absence of signs which had, moreover, overturned the anteriority of things to signs that stands in the way of cognising emptiness. In other words, the 'revolution in . . . ontological thought' he looked for had already been instituted in mathematics.

The point, then, is this. The elaboration of the code of scientific discourse in the seventeenth century to accommodate the concepts and reality of 'vacuum' and 'empty space' was a question, not of historical causation to be traced through the supposed influence of Greek atomism, but the completion of an existing semiotic paradigm. Within this discourse the terms 'vacuum' or 'empty space' were obliged to signify the absence of what before them had been conceived as full, indivisible and all-pervasively present: the plenum of breathable air and the plenum of material (as opposed to divine) existence. And, as we have seen, to write the mathematical symbol 0 is to signify the absence of the positive number signs; the absence, that is, of the unit 1 and its iterates 11, 111, 1111, etc., the absence, in other words, of entities perceived as full, indivisible, whole, integer. Democritus' embrace of the void offered seventeenth century thinkers not so much a means of thinking about 'nothing' in a new way as a classical imprimatur to a mode of thinking that they already, unknowingly, possessed.

HEBREW NOTHING

How was 'nothing' and God's creation out of the original nothing cognised within Jewish thought? To pursue this it is first necessary to recognise the split within Jewish theological discourse between morality and metaphysics, the division between the philosophical rationalism of rabbinical study fixated upon the interpretation of the Law in relation to spiritual duties and pleasures, and the esoteric doctrines of Jewish mysticism preoccupied with the Godhead, with ecstasy, with oblivion, with what is infinite and unknowable.

Classical rabbinical commentary, concerned before all else with textual interpretation of the Torah, with uncovering the meaning of God's word in order to elucidate the moral injunctions and rewards of blessings and *mitzvah*, was fragmented and scholastic: a disputatious, repetitive, hair-splitting and endlessly argumentative maze of commentaries upon commentaries upon God's word. What emerges about the notion of 'nothing' from this scholasticism is very little; or rather, very little different from that already observed with Christian scholastic theology. The orthodox rabbinical tradition seems not to have moved outside debates between neo-Platonism and Aristotelianism and the obscure impasses these gave rise to concerning God's attributes and what could, or rather could not, be said about Him. Thus, to take a single example, when Moses Maimonides, the most illustrious of Jewish scholastics, was asked: how was it possible to speak of God being alive, when to do so was to deny Him the attribute of death and therefore imply a limitation in His infinite being? His answer was to foreclose (just as Aquinas, whom he influenced, foreclosed) on the issue of 'nothing' through the trick of negative affirmation. God was simply the opposite of all that was negative; he was, in Maimonides' static anticipation of Hegel's formula, 'the negation of negation'.

Talmudic moralism did not concern itself with eschatological ultimates such as the 'beginning', 'end,' the 'infinite', 'nothing'. Cosmological knowledge of the entire universe and cosmogenic speculation about its coming into being, were foreign to the assumptions of its hermetic realism, its peculiarly rabbinical fixation on interpreting the written biblical word as the Word of God, as a sign with a referent and a meaning existing outside of, anterior to, and independent of itself. Certainly, the commitment of rabbinical hermeneutics to this anteriority in its search for the meaning behind His word, was not fertile ground for the articulation of meta-signs for 'nothing', since, as we have seen, such signs both cause and require the overturning of this anteriority in order to come into being. Neither were the rabbis prepared to compromise; though they did not set up any apparatus for the persecution of heretics beyond that of outright excommunication, their dismissal of those that pursued metaphysics was simple and extreme. For example:

> Whosoever speculated on these four things, it were better for him if he had not come into the world – what is above? what is beneath? what was beforetime? and what will be hereafter?
>
> (Quoted in Bloom, 1975, p. 51)

As one would expect, it was not within the confines of this obsessional moral realism but in the metaphysical speculation of the Kabbalah, the oral and written tradition of Jewish esoteric mystical thought, with its rituals of wonderment and formulas of awe at God's endless splendour, His infinite presence, that infinity and 'nothing' came to be signified. But speculative mysticism in itself guarantees no necessary or adequate cognising of 'nothing'. Indeed, in the 1000 year period of mainly oral transmission that preceded the eruption of Kabbalistic texts in the thirteenth century Kabbalistic thought seems to have avoided 'nothing' in favour of a more or less neo-Platonist fixation on God's monolithic, unruptured, full and ineffable presence. Within this 'throne' or 'chariot' mysticism God was infinitely distant from Man and language. He was the holy of holies, almighty, wise beyond wisdom, transcendent, king of kings, seated implacably and unapproachably on His throne in the seventh and final heaven, a centre of pure being radiating an unbearable and unnameable presence, untainted by negativity, loss, absence or that which comes from what is not: an infinite alien plenum.

This unbroken wholeness changed with the emergence of the *Zohar* Kabbalah of Moses de Leon in Spain in the late thirteenth century. It was this work, whose influence on Jewish thought was, according to Scholem (1941, p. 153), that of a 'a canonical text, which for a period of several centuries actually ranked with the Bible and the Talmud', in which an explicit signifying of 'nothing' occurred for the first time.

De Leon's Kabbalah is a vast, rambling medieval omnium – unsystematised, digressive, anecdotal, homilectic, polymorphous – of thirteenth century Jewish (principally anti-rabbinical) fixations and repressions. It is pre-occupied with Gnostic speculations about, for example, the evil left hand of God; antagonistic to any notion of confrontation or numinous union with God; uninterested in the idea of messianic return; and filled with stories, parables, homilies, enigmas illuminating the ultimate nature of the Godhead, the fate of the soul after death, the inner mystery of the Talmud revealed by number and Hebrew letter magic, the possibility of dialogues between God and the soul, the limits of meditation on God's essence through His secret names, the account of His presence in a world self-created from some original 'nothing'.

Within all this only the last item, the theosophical scheme of God's absence and presence, concerns us; it runs, in crude summary, something like the following. The universe is split between the relative and the absolute. The relative world – all that lives, dies, moves, acts, perceives, and is, the material world of nature, the senses, physical being, consciousness, history – is governed by a single transvasive figure, common to the whole Kabbalah, called the Tree of Life (Illustration 21).

The Tree of Life is the diagram of creation, a figure which depicts, iconically models, and, at the same time, reveals the dynamic of God as originator. In the *Zohar* the figure comes alive in the resonances produced by its ten outer nodes – the *sephiroth* – vibrating and impinging on each other as the divine impulse passes through them. Despite their given names the *sephiroth* are not, of course, personifications nor reified human attributes. They are the reverse: the nodes are themselves names, signs, aspects of God, points at which God's immanence can be signified, and their linguistic labels merely human attributes which image them.

What then does the *Zohar* say about the Tree of Life as a figure of God's creative presence? Specifically, how does God make the tree, and indeed any real and natural tree in the relative world, create its fruit? What, in other words, is the connecting medium, between the absolute of God and the relative world we all inhabit? How, in terms of mundane humanly understandable causality, does the divine impulse enter the tree?

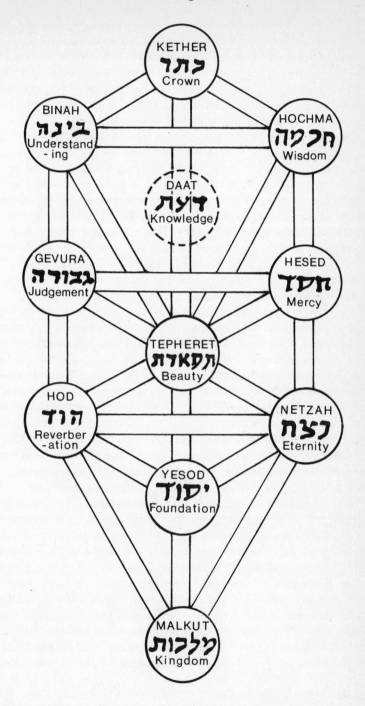

Illustration 21 The Tree of Life.

Among the nodes, *kether*, the supreme crown is distinguished from the other nine as the origin and channel, the vehicle through which God's influence flows. Below the crown the other *sephiroth* form an inverted tree of emanation receiving and transvecting what, for them, originates in the crown. The *kether* is precisely the creative principle, the place of entry or point of impact of the divine lightening flash which activates the tree. It is thus ambiguously a part of life, within all that lives: and at the same time other-worldly, outside of life, the sign of an invisible, originating and immanent God. Beyond *kether* lies the veil of *ain soph aur*, limitless endless light, beyond that *ain soph*, the veil of infinity or limitlessness itself, and beyond that *ain*, the void, nothing, emptiness – the absolute – where God, as pure declarative presence, He who utters to Moses *I am that I am*, is manifested. *Kether* is thus the origin of being, the place where something comes to exist *out of nothing*. If the other nine *sephiroth* are signs, marks of God's attributes in the living world, then it is a meta-sign: a sign for the absence of any presence other than that which comes from 'nothing'.

One can express this distinction between the *kether* and the other nodes in secular and formal terms without using a semiotic vocabulary. Thus Harold Bloom in his eassay *Kabbalah and Criticism*, which is devoted entirely to the proposition that the Kabbalah can be interpreted as a 'theory of influence' in which the *sephiroth* are the fundamental principles of poesis, the modes by which language attains literary significance, identifies *kether* as the 'paradoxical idea of influence itself' (Bloom, 1975, p. 29). And in observing that 'the irony of all influence, initially, is that the source is emptied out into a state of absence, in order for the receiver to accomodate the influx of apparent being', he converts what for us is an essential meta-lingual ambiguity, the inevitable oscillation between presence and absence inherent in any meta-sign of origination, into a site of paradoxical irony.

Is the *kether* a theosophical zero? Certainly 'crown', indicating something at the edge or physical limit of spatial extension, together with 'hollow crown', and occasionally 'fundamental point', with their direct iconographic connections to zero through rings, circles and the minimal graphic presence of a dot, are suggestive. As is the topological sense in the picture of *kether* as a boundaried enclosure, window, an aperture, a hole through which divine lightening enters the world of relative existence from the absolute. Moreover, *kether* exhibits the same semiotic functions as zero. Both in a global context, as a meta-sign for that which issues from 'nothing', it disrupts the neo-Platonic and fundamentally Gothic theosophical code of *Merkabbah* mysticism, and locally, as an element in the sign-producing network that forms the Tree of Life, it has a unique initiating position, distinguished from the other nodes by being the creative origin of the whole *sephirotic* system.

The *kether*, then, looks and acts like a zero sign within the *Zohar*. In the *Book of Creation*, the oracular, cryptic Kabbalistic work which marks the

beginning of the millennium of oral tradition terminated by Spanish Kab-
balism, the *sephiroth* appeared simply and literally as *numbers*, relics,
perhaps, of Pythagorean numerology; and zero was certainly not one of
them. How these numbers were transmuted during the oral phase of Kab-
balism into signs and names of God in the *Zohar* is obscure. But one can
imagine the impact of zero on them through the matrix of external historical
circumstance. Like those who cognised the vacuum and empty space in the
seventeenth century, the men who produced the works of Spanish Kab-
balism in the thirteenth century did not exist in a semiotic void in relation to
the idea of 'nothing'. The opposite was the case. The twelfth and thirteenth
centuries were the golden period of Arab–Jewish collaborative culture, the
period which saw the transmission of works on arab mathematics and
science and Hindu numerals from Spain to Christian Europe; works which
the Jews, among many others, were instrumental in translating. As linguistic, cultural middlemen Jewish intellectuals could hardly have been unres-
ponsive to the semiotic novelty, or unscathed by the disruptive ferment, of
the ideas they were passing on. In particular, the idea of zero.

From what has been said, it would be perverse to deny that zero – sign for
the absence of the nine signs 1, . . . ,9 – and *kether* – sign for the absence of
the nine *sephiroth* – are parallel semiotic configurations. This can be con-
cluded without any need to claim that the Supreme Crown was conceived to
be 'equal' in any sense to zero. In fact, given that *kether* was the principal and
highest of the ten nodes in a system of thought that set so much store in
numerological manipulation, its identity as a 'number', would most
naturally have been ten written not, of course, as Roman X but as Hindu 10,
an enigmatic and magically charged juxtaposition of the ancient unit,
the full, indivisible, totally present, enthroned God, and *ain*, the absent,
originating 'nothing'.

Finally, recall from the earlier discussion of meta-signs how the semiotic
action of zero was seen to be inseparable from, and indeed coterminous
with, the emergence of a new, self-conscious, subject; a subject who, by
initiating the activity of counting, produces the numbers as the discrete
written traces of its presence. According to Scholem's exegesis, de Leon's
Kabbalah exhibits the emergence, witnessed as a progressive differentiation
of pronouns for God, of just such a subject:

> God in the most deeply hidden of His manifestations, when he has as it
> were just decided to launch upon His work of Creation, is called HE. God
> in the complete unfolding of his Being, Grace, and Love, in which HE
> becomes capable of being perceived . . . and therefore of being expressed,
> is called YOU. But God, in His supreme manifestation, where the fullness
> of His Being finds its final expression in the last and all-embracing of His
> attributes, is called I. This is the stage of true individuation in which God
> as a person says I to Himself. This Divine Self, this I, . . . [is] the presence

and immanence of God in the whole of Creation. It is the point where man, in attaining the deepest understanding of his own self, becomes aware of the presence of God.

(Scholem, 1941, p. 212)

This differentiation of subjectivity allows the Kabbalistic account of *ex nihilo* creation to turn in on itself: the creation of something out of nothing, of the immanent self-conscious I from the He of the original void, is, as Scholem (1941, p. 213) expresses, it the 'external aspect of something which takes place in God Himself'. Thus the figure of *kether* becomes in the Kabbalah a sign for autocthony, an iconic diagrammatic token of God's creation of Himself and of the world out of the absolute of nothing.

KING LEAR AND 'NOTHING'

Whatever its role at the centre of Moses de Leon's theosophic scheme, zero's impact on European consciousness from the thirteenth century was plainly not through the Kabbalah, but in an obvious and direct way as a number: as a Hindu numeral in the arithmetic of money, and as the principle of zero balance in the double-entry book-keeping that controlled the expanding market of credit, debt, and commodities engendered by mercantile capitalism.

The disruption and moral disintegration inherent in capitalism's threat to commoditise social reality, its capacity to nihilise fellow feeling and reduce human beings to acquisitive wolves fixated on money and power, is the central theme of two plays, Jonson's *Volpone* and Shakespeare's *King Lear*, written a year of each other in London around 1605.

Both playrights would have learned about numbers at school some thirty years earlier, and were in the first generation of children in England to have learned about zero from Robert Recorde's *Arithmetic*, which bases itself on a strange pedagogical mixture of the new decimal notation and the old abacus manipulations. And they wrote their plays at the historical point of transition between two methods of writing down monetary accounts: when the new Hindu numerals based on zero and the traditional abacus-based Roman ones about to be ousted by them existed, briefly, side by side, until the eclipse of Roman numerals signalled the death of a feudal classical order and the arrival of the accounting practices, and the commoditised reality of mercantile capitalism.

Both plays dramatise reductions to nothing, charting the annihilation of human warmth, the dissolution of social, natural, familial bonds, the emptying of kindness, sympathy, tenderness, love, pity, affection into hollow shells, into substitutes for themselves which take part in the deal, the transaction, the exchange. Jonson's play – a satire rooted in the social immediacy and cultural details of its milieu – confronts 'nothing' as a pre-determined moral and social given, the depraved end-point of the moral scale occupied by pure 'inhuman', vulpine, greed. Focusing on the social route to 'nothing' through all the literal and palpable details of gold, money, and the manipulations thereof, *Volpone* does not and does not need to interest itself in the metaphysics of 'nothing', in the nature of annihilation and of being 'nothinged' *per se.*

Shakespeare's interest in 'nothing' (like Donne's and like that of the *nihil* paradoxists of the sixteenth century) was more intellectually alert, allusive, and linguistically abstract than Jonson's. And more varied: from the comic play on nothing/vagina in *Much Ado About Nothing* and in Hamlet's savaging of Ophelia in *Hamlet*, to the fixation on Time's nothing – oblivion – and the self's ambitious ascent into nothing, on the 'absence, darkness, death; things which are not' in *Macbeth*, to nothing begetting nothing in *King Lear*, whose *ex nihilo nihil fit*, is given the lie by human love being annihilated and counted out of existence by all that comes from 'nothing'.

The action of the play opens with Lear old, wishing to crawl unburdened to his grave, about to play out a promissory deal, a transactional charade, whose unreal premise involves an exchange of material goods for spoken signs: he will hand over portions of his kingdom – land, goods, the privileges, prerogatives and exercise of royal power – to each of his daughters in exchange for formulaic utterances, set empty speeches of love for him. In this opening scene Lear is contriving to absent himself, to dissolve a certain feudal self, to annihilate the unitary, gothic self of his kinghood, by selling it; transacting it in precisely those terms alien to it.

Lear: . . . which of you shall we say doth love us most that we our largest bounty may extend.

                                                                (I(i)52)

The demand of 'most' for 'largest', the maximum amount of love for a, ceremoniously,measurable portion of the kingdom, reveals that it is in the one-dimensional language of quantity – arithmetic – that Lear has constructed his deal. It is a deal which treats love as a commodity, something to be bought and sold by suitably formulated speech: speech fashioned so as not to 'mar. . .fortunes', speech that had internalised the principle of the deal to become the language of commerce.

Goneral and Regan render him – in language that is obsequious, mechanically filled with comparatives and superlatives of quantity, transparently duplicitous to the audience if not to Lear – the verbal formula he seems to want. He is made to appear satisfied: they immediately get their portions. Cordelia, appalled and emptied by the cynical ease of her sisters' lies, can neither signify her love in this way, nor withdraw and refuse the transaction, nor remain silent:

Lear:	. . . what can you say to draw a third more opulent than you sisters? Speak.
Cordelia:	Nothing my lord.
Lear:	Nothing?
Cordelia:	Nothing.
Lear:	Nothing will come out of nothing: speak again.

(I(i)90)

No encounter with *King Lear* could miss the force and threat of such a 'nothing,' or avoid the ominous warnings of disruption, the promise of violent explosion it sends echoing through the play. From Cordelia's 'nothing', and its double in the sub-plot uttered by Edmund, the action and the themes of this tragedy bitterly and relentlessly unfold: Kent is instantly nullified, banished. Cordelia is repudiated, robbed, disowned, and ultimately hanged. Gloucester, Lear's aged double, is sadistically blinded. And Lear is riven apart, by a great arc of reason-filled madness, and dies at the very moment he faces his blindness to 'nothing'. The play shows the destruction of a world and a self by a force derived from 'nothing'; a force wearing the mask, as we shall see, of zero.

In forcing Cordelia to outbid her sisters Lear coerces her into the world of exchangeable commodities where, before the play has started, he has trapped himself. Cordelia's attempt at silence comes from the intuition that any answer to Lear's question would make sense only in a world where love, as she has to understand it, is absent. But, unlike the Fool who can make mock of the difference between silence and saying nothing, the moral space she occupies precludes any doubleness. She cannot voice this absence; she can only say 'nothing'.

Cordelia is made to stand for, embody, and, throughout the play, never depart from a conception of natural love as love in *action*, in kinship, in context, in use, in obligation, in mutual responsibility. Shakespeare puts it all into the verbs:

Cordelia:	You have begot me, bred me, lov'd me I
	Return those duties back as are right fit
	Obey you, love you, and most honour you.

(I(i)98)

These verbs express the domestic pieties of the classic and gothic, pre-Renaissance, world. A world under threat, within which love takes place through lived action; it recreates itself through obligations, duties, promises, and contracts of nurture. Such love is *produced*, and has meaning only *in situ*, in the context of its production. Lear's transaction, by arithmetising it, by forcefully inserting into it a system of mercantile exchange and making it an object of deals, replaces this produced love, the continuous result of a lived practice, which is how Cordelia conceives it, by love neutralised into a *commodity*, an item within a system of measurable values. And in doing so rapes it.

It is this violation, this destruction that *King Lear* relentlessly and obsessively pursues. The play was written in a London of bubonic plague, cheap death, religious burnings, torture; a London given over to the deal: the buy/sell transactions of a risingly brutal capitalism dealing in information through spies and informers, flesh through rampantly exploitative prostitution, liberty and freedom through indentures and slavery. It sets up, and ultimately recoils in horror from, what it conceives to be the terminal transaction: the buying and selling of natural love.

For Cordelia, confronted with Lear's question about love ('how much?') the only response, the only one possible in her moral universe, is silence. Her 'nothing', her failed attempt to remain silent, to stay outside the language of commodities set up by Lear, becomes for him an answer – the arithmetically worst answer – to his question. Obsessed by the need to close his deal Lear converts Cordelia's unarticulated refusal to bid – a meta-sign about deals which she has not the means to express – into a bid.

What Lear, blind to the difference between silence and saying nothing, between a sign and a sign about signs, has to be made to see is the nature of Cordelia's 'nothing'. His education into the meaning of 'nothing' is through numbers. He is given two lessons in the arithmetic of nothing; first by the Fool, who serves as Cordelia's moral and intellectual surrogate, and then by his other two daughters. Both lessons end on zero.

The first reference to Lear's Fool, pining for Cordelia, establishes him as her proxy, her advocate in the case of 'nothing'. He begins by teasing Lear with a piece of doggerel, a commonplace *nihil* skit which, by quantifying the world out of existence and ending on the request for nothing, allusively mocks the whole arithmetical language and fate of Lear's deal.

Fool: Mark it, Nuncle:
           Have more than thou showest
           Speak less than thou knowest
           Lend less than thou owest
           Ride more than thou goest
           Learn more than thou trowest
           Set less than thou throwest
           Leave thy drink and thy whore
           And keep in-a-door
           And thou shalt have more
           than two tens to a score.

                                                            (I(iv)133)

Kent, as straight man, answers:

Kent: This is nothing fool.

(I(iv)134)

Then the Fool twits Lear directly:

Fool: Can you make no use of nothing Nuncle?

(I(iv)138)

Lear, oblivious to the Fool's line of attack, still anaesthetised to the import and significance of Cordelia's 'nothing', repeats his formula from the opening scene:

Lear: Why, no, boy; nothing can be made out of nothing.

(I(iv)139)

Lear's foolish, uncomprehending repetition proves unbearable to the Fool, who explodes into scorn, and taunts Lear into being a bitter fool. Then the Fool returns to 'nothing' tracing its shape from an egg to a coin to a crown to Lear's bald, empty, head. Then, more explicitly, with a growing satirical edge, an emptied place:

Fool: I'd rather be any kind of thing than a fool; and yet I would not be thee Nuncle. Thou has pared thy wits on both sides and left nothing in the middle

(I(iv)192)

And finally, in the terminal and terminating barb:

Fool: Thou art an O without a figure. I am better than thou art now; I am a fool, thou art nothing.

(I(iv)202)

Lear is reduced to a zero and to nothing. And as a last flourish on the difference between a sign for silence and silence, the difference between saying nothing and saying 'nothing', he turns to Goneril:

Fool: Yes, forsooth, I will hold my tongue; so your face bids me though you say nothing.

(I(iv)204)

It is now the turn of Goneril and Regan to diminish Lear to zero. Where the Fool was satirical, allusive, allegorical, Goneril is viscious and immediate. She vilifies the remnant of Lear's kinghood – his entourage of one hundred knights and squires – as a brothel rabble, and suggests, in arithmetically icy language, that he 'disquantity' it. Goneril and Regan start to systematically contract Lear's kinghood, to disquantity it by numerical shrinkage: they halve his train of one hundred to fifty, and then again to twenty-five. At this point Lear perceives, bitterly, for the first time, that he might be a victim of the very language of commodities he has instituted.

Lear: Thy fifty doth double five and twenty
                 And thou art twice her love.

                                                                        (II(iv)262)

Made to bid for *himself*, to turn himself into an object of commerce, he begins to fear the Fool's *nihil*, the disintegration of himself, the self-dissolution, that lies at the end of this arithmetic reduction. Goneril and Regan leave him in no suspense: from one hundred they move swiftly through fifty, twenty-five, ten, one, and then with

Regan: What need one?

                                                                        (I(iv)265)

Lear arrives at zero. Thus the language of arithmetic, in which his train of followers is counted down to nothing, and in which the Fool articulates the loss of Lear's kinghood as a thing reduced to zero, becomes the vehicle and image of the destruction of Lear's self and of natural love. Both, by being converted into number signs, are emptied, neutered, stripped of human content. After this Lear knows he will go mad. And when he does, his first release is to rage with demented fixation on the 'need' denied him by Regan, the need for gratitude, for companionship, for justice and the need which he has murdered and cannot ask for, the need for 'natural' human love; needs which now count for nothing in a world where 'What need one?' reduces human beings to dumb creatures, to isolated pre-social nothings.

Cordelia's 'nothing' which detonates Lear's reduction to madness and zero is reproduced – to the word – in the sub-plot of the play, where again it initiates a chain that ends in inhumanity and violence. Edmund, feigning brotherly protectiveness, pretends to conceal a letter he has written, supposedly from his brother Edgar, which reveals Edgar as plotting against their father Gloucester:

Gloucester: What paper are you reading.
Edmund: Nothing my lord.
Gloucester: No? What needed then that terrible dispatch of it into your
                    pocket. The quality of nothing hath not such need to hide itself.
                    Let's see: come; if it be nothing I shall not need spectacles.

                                                                        (I(ii)35)

Indeed he will not need spectacles, for his eyes will be gouged out before he can see the treachery of Edmund's 'nothing'. Edmund is a Machiavel, ruthless, fast, self-made from nothing. His origin is a void: a bastard, conceived outside sanctioned kin, a whore's son, whose mother, his 'natural' beginning, the play reduces to an empty vaginal hole – a nothing – as 'dark and viscious' as Gloucester's eye sockets will become.

Lear's madness, made hot by the fantasy of revenge, comes to be dominated by an all-devouring obsession with sexual generation. And it rides him on a journey that ends in death and the emptiness of an inhuman, mechanical repetition. His call for revenge is cloaked at first in the language of justice. He sets up a mock trial of Goneril and Regan, but is unable to finish it – to do so would be to visit the origin, the initiating 'nothing' of his own madness. This he cannot do, and so is condemned to go on, reproducing its consequences blindly, without human purpose, until he finds his sons-in-law and has his suitably mechanical, mindless, and repetitive revenge of 'kill, kill, kill, kill, kill, kill'.

Sexual generation starts with copulation:

Lear: I pardon that man's life. What was thy cause?
             Adultery?
             Thou shalt not die: die for adultery. No:
             The wren goes to 't and the small gilded fly
             Does lecher in my sight.
             Let copulation thrive

                                                        (IV(vi)117)

By accusing birds and insects of adultery – patently absurd – Lear is being made to grasp at the distinction between sanctioned, lawful, 'natural' sexuality, and the uncontrolled lust of copulation. But he is unable to separate the two, instead they are joined in the figure of a centaur: half the gods' inheritance, half the sulphorous pit. The image is unstable, the pit swallows the rest, and Lear ends in an invective of disgust and revulsion at the stench of the female part (the smell of nothing) and of mortality. Where earlier, in the sonnets, Shakespeare saw lust, however destructive, as part of the human moral order, an expense of spirit in a waste of shame, he portrays it here as dehumanised and empty. Sexuality, reduced to no more than the urgent quivering of a fly, shrinks to mindless vibration, a blind animal urge to repeat in a world where the loss of human love makes anything else impossible. And procreation is dead, replaced by an unnatural grotesque continuation, replicating ingratitude, hate, and lifelessness. Lear will have no grandchildren, no 'natural' continuation, no issue from a site he has already cursed:

Lear: Into her womb convey sterility
            Dry up in her the organs of increase
            And from her derogate body never spring
            A babe to honour her.

                                              (I(iv)287)

The two great themes of *King Lear*, human blindness to itself, to love, and the horror of *ex nihil*, of that which issues from nothing, are reflected and doubled between the plot and the sub-plot. Cordelia and Edgar, both legitimate heirs, both innocent, both loved, maligned, repudiated, usurped, banished, both witnessing the seeing and unseeing madness of their fathers, are mirror reflections of the same 'natural' love. Likewise Edmund's literal bastardy finds its image, and sexual confirmation, in the unnatural daughterhood, the figurative bastardy of Goneril and Regan. Lear's metaphorical blindness to the literal 'nothing' wrenched from Cordelia, which fills the play, is the invisible double of Gloucester's staged, full view, all too literal, blinding engendered by Edmund's 'nothing'.

Lear's metaphorical blindness is also a blindness to metaphor. He cannot 'see' the ambiguity of Cordelia's 'nothing', he is blind to the difference between a meta-sign whose meaning is to deny the possibility of speaking and the literal spoken sign 'nothing'. Harshly dramatised in his separation from Cordelia and the reduction of his kinghood to zero, this ambiguity returns, inverted and softened, late in the play when Lear is briefly united with Cordelia. He woos her with a strange and moving domestic fantasy:

Lear: ... come, let's away to prison;
            We two alone will sing like birds i' the cage
            When thou dost ask me blessing, I'll kneel down,
            And ask of three forgiveness: so we'll live,
            And pray, and sing, and tell old tales, and laugh
            At gilded butterflies, and hear poor rogues
            Talk of court news; and we'll talk with them too,
            Who loses and who wins; who's in and who's out;
            And take upon's the mystery of things,
            As if we were God's spies: and we 'll wear out,
            In a walled prison, packs and sects of great ones
            That ebb and flow by th'moon.

                                        (V(iii)19)

The dream Lear offers Cordelia is the presence-in-absence of ghosts. Protected from the ravages of the world, the machinations of power and the passing of time, enclosed in a mythical and benign mutuality, distanced from others and from their selves as spies for an absent God, they will exist in an unreal stasis, as ambiguous signs of signs, living by proxy, both in life and at one remove from life – on a meta-level – through the gossip and court news that make up the spoken signs of life.

The play ends with an address:

Edgar:　　The weight of this sad time we must obey;
　　　　　　Speak what we feel, and not what we ought to say.
　　　　　　The oldest hath borne most: we that are young
　　　　　　Shall never see so much, nor live so long.

(V(iii)326)

Who are the 'we' here? Read as a conventional tragic coda pointing inwards to the dramatic events, 'this sad time' is the fictional time created by the play, and the 'we' signifies the generation left on stage – those whose lives pale before that of their tragic king.

But there is also an external reading: one can interpret the final address as pointing outwards to make 'this sad time' the early seventeenth century time of its original performance, and 'the young' those that issued from that time; so that the 'we' in the first two lines indicates the remaining characters left to uphold the pieties of natural feeling, while the 'we that are young' points to the unknown future, to those who will never experience these events but must live in the historical wake of those times.

One can, in other words, follow the lead given by the Fool earlier in the play when he 'predicts', as Shakespeare's *contemporary*, that

Fool,　　　... the realm of Albion
　　　　　　Come to great confusion:
　　　　　　Then comes the time, who lives to see't,
　　　　　　That going shall be us'd with feet.
　　　　　　This prophecy Merlin shall make; for I live
　　　　　　before his time.

(III(iii)95)

and allow the play to step out of its own mythical time into history. In this case Lear is not a pagan folk king mythologised by Shakespeare, nor some trans-historical figure of nihilism, nor the hero of a Christian epic of Job-like redemption, nor the universal Old Dying Man Goethe took him to be, he is the embodiment of a contemporary, historically unique, social and cultural event. Lear registers, he acts out, he is, the rupture in the medieval world brought about by the transactions of Renaissance capitalism. Read thus, the play is Shakespeare's encounter with the empty doubleness of 'nothing', with the spectre that he saw in those transactions; saw not in terms of abstract meta-signs or some grand metaphysical void but as zero, painfully concretised in the buying and selling of kinghood, self and love through numbers.

4

Absence of an Origin

For Lear the question: 'What need one?' is an open wound that cannot be healed. As the rhetorical origin of his madness, the question's answer – zero – becomes the name of his condition and the means by which he is reduced to a cypher, to the nothing that comes from nothing; zero is an image, a sign outside 'natural' language, that points to a source of horror that, for Lear, is unsayable. In the twentieth century where Nothing comes ubiquitously into its all too sayable own, where moral, intellectual, theological, artistic, and cultural vacuums have each spawned their own insistent nihilisms, such a unified and particular image for emptiness and nothing seems no longer possible. None the less, though zero is no longer an alien sign, the mask of an inhuman otherness worn by mercantile capitalism that it was for Shakespeare, but a commonplace constituent of speech, the figures it produces – degree zero, zero countdown, zero-sum game, absolute zero, zero option, ground zero – still convey a charge of absence, origination, finality, annihilation, the sense of a beyond which nothing which permeates its iconographic associations.

And what in the early seventeenth century was metaphorised in tragedy returns in the twentieth century naked in melodrama. The metaphor is literalised into a name: the central character of Elmer Rice's expressionist melodrama, *The Adding Machine*, is called, with a simple blank directness, Zero. He is not a noble figure, a king writ tragically large, but a banal nobody, a dull and obscure everyman, an annihilated self whose life is to be nothing, to achieve nothing, and to leave nothing behind. A grotesque and dramatically lurid wage slave of industrial capitalism, Zero evacuates his days meaninglessly adding up columns of numbers. Sacked to make way for a mechanical adding machine, he murders his boss, dies, is tried, goes to paradise, enjoys a brief transcendent moment of knowing and love – only to learn that he must return to life, as he has returned before and will do so again, washed clean of love and of all he has learned, to live another zero existence operating the adding machine of modern, 1923, capitalism.

The melodrama (if that is the form it will be) of the contemporary adding machine, the computer, has yet to be written. Certainly the form of capitalism the computer engenders is no longer confined to the arena of wage slaves, it is no longer mechanico-industrial but electronic and financial. Financial capitalism is distinguished by the buying and selling not merely of goods, labour, and services but of money. Money which in order to transact itself has to be of a radically new kind. Now changes in money are, as we have seen, intimately connected to the semiotic medium in which it is counted and accounted. And since both the language and logical structure of computers privilege zero in a very profound way, it is reasonable to expect that a phenomenon recognisable in terms of zero will be at the centre of the shift in money signs that constitutes the emergence of financial capitalism. It is also reasonable to expect that radical shifts in other Western codes contemporary with the emergence of financial capitalism will echo its transformation of the structure of money signs. To pursue this expectation I shall discuss first the economic code in which the new money occurs and then, in the light of this, the code of written language in which, so it is claimed, a new form of text, a change in 'writing' itself, must be recognised.

XENOMONEY

It was in the early 1970s that a fundamental shift took place in the financial practices that underpin and create the circulation of money-signs. What occurred then was an historically unique confluence and structural integration of four separate monetary phenomena, none of which was novel, but which together created a multi-billion dollar a day global money market and a radically new highly volatile, world monetary order. A realistic description of the workings of these phenomena – *floating* rates of exchange, an *inconvertible* world currency, the growth of *off-shore* money in the Euromarkets, the emergence of secondary markets in *financial futures/options* contracts – would need much esoteric discussion that lies far outside the scope of this book. However, the phenomena themselves, forming the basis as they do of widespread commercial and market practices, are operationally simple. Moreover, from the present perspective interested in identifying changes in money as a *sign*, only their semiotic characteristics need be explicated.

The present world currency is *de facto* the United States dollar. What is a dollar? What sorts of money signs are called dollars? What, to reach for the most palpable and concrete, a piece of paper, does a one dollar bill signify?

A dollar bill is an item of paper money, a written promissory note issued by the United States Treasury to an unnamed bearer. Promising what? In terms of our earlier discussion, paper money guarantees absent but potentially recoverable specie and, until 1973, such was the dollar's promise. The US government had formally obliged its Treasury to deliver 1/35th of an ounce of gold on receipt of a dollar bill if the bearer of the bill so requested. In short the dollar was a convertible currency: one dollar could be converted into a specific amount of some anterior 'thing' – gold – which was held to have a fixed, unchangeable, intrinsic value. In 1973, after much crisis ridden confusion and financial turmoil in the wake of the Vietnam war and amid the moves which led to the four-fold increase in world oil prices, the US government cancelled its self-imposed obligation to deliver specie. The dollar was cut loose from any fixed equivalence with gold (or indeed anything else): a dollar bill presented to the US Treasury entitled the holder to an identical replacement of itself. As a promissory note it became a tautological void. The dollar became, in other words, an inconvertible currency with no intrinsic internal value whose extrinsic value with respect to other currencies was allowed to float in accordance with market forces.

Thus a dollar's 'value', what traditionally as a paper money sign it is supposed to signify to its bearer, becomes what it is worth on a day-to-day basis to those who hold it. Inside the United States, as on-shore money proclaiming itself in circulation as 'legal tender', its value is whatever goods, necessarily priced in dollars, it will purchase. Outside the United States, circulating as off-shore money in the so-called Euromarkets, its value is whatever goods the local currency exchanged for it will buy. Within this simple formulation of a dollar's value there are two fundamental points that need elaboration. The first concerns the nature of the Euromarket, in particular, the relation, in terms of signs, between on-shore dollars and off-shore Eurodollars. The second relates to the fact that characterising the value of a dollar, what it signifies as a money-sign, in terms of its momentary exchange-worth inserts a radically new time-bound element into what is meant by the term 'money'.

Off-shore money, that is money of a country held outside that country or by a foreign bank inside the country, has been a feature of commercial life since at least the sixteenth century in Europe and much longer elsewhere. It was not uncommon, for example, in the commercial centres of Europe of that period for foreign currencies (Ducats in London, Sovereigns in Amsterdam) to circulate freely alongside the home currency providing the means to denominate and settle transactions. In its modern incarnation it appears in the mid-twentieth century as the Eurodollar, since it was in Europe and in dollars that the present global money market has its origin and initial development. The market is said to have started in the early 1950s when the Soviet Union, fearing that the USA might freeze deposits of Soviet dollars held in US banks, transferred its dollars out of the United States to the European banks who still trade them today. The market in these and other foreign held dollars grew rapidly, principally through banks in London. First, multiplicatively through the 1960s, then exponentially in the 1970s as banks in London started to on-lend the billions of dollars of extra revenues deposited with them by the newly rich oil producers to third world borrowers. It has continued growing to the present by facilitating more of the same – globally recycling credit from medium-term surplus trade balances into long-term debts.

For 'Euro' and 'dollars' one should write 'xeno' and 'money' respectively. The Eurodollar has long since shed its attachment to Europe. It is, in fact, no longer geographically located but circulates within an electronic global market which, though still called the Eurodollar market, is now *the* international capital market. And its attachment to dollars is denominational rather than actual: not only can all currencies be swapped instantaneously in and out of the dollar, but there is also a growing volume of other instruments within this new market, such as Eurobonds, issued in Yen, Deutschemarks, Ecus and so on.

As a mechanism for recycling financial imbalances (petrodollars in the 1970s, Japanese and German trade surpluses in the 1980s) the Euromarket has been highly instrumental in increasing the stock of world debt. Critics of the market point out that while debt in itself is not undesirable, since capitalism could not function without it, the quality of Euromarket debt and the underlying reason for its production by the market is the source of a dangerous, possibly fatal, flaw in the world monetary order.

The quality of a debt concerns the possibility of its default. Any debt has risk attached to it: one can always imagine real circumstances under which money lent will not be repaid. What is of interest to the lender is the *prior calculation* of such risk based, obviously, on the lender's reading of the borrower's financial status. If this reading fails to take place, if for example there is a baffle between creditor and debtor masking the latter, an intervening mechanism that separates the source and destination of the money being transferred, then the borrower and lender will be unknown to each other and the rational assessment of risk by the lender will be impaired: with the consequence that the propensity to bad debt will increase. The Eurodollar market, by allowing debts to be spread, split up, swapped, syndicated, traded and reassigned, provides precisely such an intervening and anonymising mechanism. 'We are all joined together in one long chain of credit; but we can't examine the balance sheet of every link, and we never know who the ultimate borrower is', is how one Eurobanker has described it (Davidson, 1983, p. 137).

Semiotically this masking of the borrower results in a loss of deixis, a reduction in the idexicality of money signs. Recall how in an earlier shift paper money differed from the imaginary bank money it displaced precisely in terms of such a reduction. But though it dispenses with the apparatus of signature, personal witness, and attachment to an original owner, paper money retains its domestic, national indexicality; it relies as a sign on its use within the borders and physical reality of the sovereign state whose central bank is the author of the promise it carries. In contrast, xenomoney is without history, ownerless, and without traceable national origin. If paper money insists on anonymity with respect to individual bearers but is deictically bound on the level of sovereignty, xenomoney anonymises itself with respect to individuals *and* nation states.

Not knowing ultimate borrowers and the disguising of risk such ignorance entails increases bad debt. And bad enough debt, as is well known, leads to bankruptcy, and bankruptcies lead to closures of banks, which in turn create runs on other banks, a state of monetary crisis, financial panic and total breakdown of money system. Within domestic, on-shore banking there is a traditional means of cutting short the flight into panic and financial collapse. Each domestic economy has an ultimate lender, the central bank of that sovereign state who, to stabilise its system and avoid the onset of panic, will act as the lender of last resort and underwrite, that is buy, bank debts. In the Euromarket there is no single lender of last resort. What then would be the result of a major Eurodollar default? How likely is it, on theoretical grounds, that one might occur?

Very likely, according to the authors of *The Incredible Eurodollar* (Hogan and Pearce, 1984) whose journalistic subtitle, *or why the world's money system is collapsing*, belies the seriousness with which it defends its thesis, viz. that by masking risk and allowing trade surpluses to be transformed into potentially bad debts, the Euromarket is a self-enhancing mechanism that perpetuates itself by subverting the very forces which would diminish debt and bring about the balance of world trade. There are two basic possibilities. A major default can occur, for example a 100 billion dollar debt of some sovereign state goes bad. To avert a crisis the banks who own this debt are forced to appeal to their own central banks to act as lenders of last resort. They would do so by 'rescheduling' the loan into the future, thereby deepening the debt still further with their own reserves, and so increasing the likelihood of the next default occurring. Or, the process will be slower and less explicit: debt servicing activity will gradually enlarge until it depresses 'real' commercial activity into recession. And, since world currency – the dollar in which these debts are denominated – has no *intrinsic* value, the irresistible response to this recession would be to print money. The Federal Reserve would manufacture the required number of dollars. This would lead to a worldwide increase in inflation and so deepen the recession into a commercial and monetary collapse.

Either way the scenario is dire. *The Incredible Eurodollar* offers only one, fundamentalist, solution: eliminate 'false' money, dissolve the whole institution of xenomoney, terminate the unregulated conversion of trade surplus into debt, return to bilaterally balanced trade, re-establish fixed rates of foreign exchange, and beyond all else re-introduce a monetary order based on a *convertible* world currency. In effect, the authors advocate a return to a gothic world order (Aquinas is embraced as a forebear) in which a sane monetary 'realism' based on physical goods repudiates the ontological abuse involved in the printing of money unbacked by specie, and insists on a palpable *origin*, some 'thing' with intrinsic worth, as the source of money's value. To be truly gothic, to reachieve the iconic monetary order of medieval Europe, the 'thing' would have to be gold. But metallic economies, they admit, are no longer practical. Instead, they propose a 'Commodity Pound': 'defined as an imaginary fixed basket of goods in the proportions of the weights in the cost of living index'. A solution, in other words, which requires a total and atavistic dissolution of the present-day monetary system.

Meanwhile the world monetary order rests on xenomoney, the above is just a scenario, the solution to it perhaps in the end no more than a modern Gold Bug's fantasy of return to the iconic simplicity before the onset of mercantile, industrial and now financial capitalism. We are left with the question: what, as a money sign, does xenomoney *signify*, given that it cannot identify itself in terms of some prior, intrinsically valuable icon?

In traditional terms money functions as a unit of account, a store of value, and most importantly – since this is taken to be its defining characteristic – a medium of exchange:

> Since a barter system may be very cumbersome and inefficient, it is generally found useful to have some good or token which is widely accepted as payment in settlement of debts. Goods can be exchanged for money, which can then be exchanged for other goods, and hence money serves as the medium through which exchange is facilitated.
>
> (Bannock, 1984, p. 302)

Such characterisation works through the difference between *goods*, the anterior things whose exchange money exists to facilitate, and *money*, posterior to goods and standing as a token in place of them. It breaks down and becomes semiotically counter-informative, as we observed earlier, when this distinction disappears: when money enters the category of 'goods' and is itself bought and sold through the medium of money. As both object and medium, thing and token, both a commodity and a sign for a commodity, money is a dualistic and self-reflexive sign. The duality as a manifestation of xenomoney's status as a certain kind of meta-sign will be elaborated on later. For the present one can make the self-reflexivity of money, its capacity to act as a medium of exchange for itself, the basis for what it signifies.

As a sign one can say that xenomoney, floating, and inconvertible to anything outside itself, signifies itself. More specifically, it signifies the possible relationships it can establish with future states of itself. Its 'value' is the relation between what it *was* worth, as an index number in relation to some fixed and arbitrary past state taken as an origin, and what the market judges it *will* be worth at different points in the future. For what it signifies to be a market variable, and for it to be 'futured' in this sense as a continuous time-occupying sign, xenomoney must be bought and sold in a market that monetises time; a market in which there exist financial instruments that, by commoditising the difference between the value of present money (spot rate) and its future value (forward rate), allow 'money' to have a single time-bound identity. In the early 1970s, the appropriate instruments, that is trade-able financial futures and options contracts, came into prominence in the Chicago Financial Futures Market.

Futures and options contracts in themselves are not new: the forward buying and selling of currency in the foreign exchange markets, and the forward buying and selling of physical commodities (grain and meat in mid-nineteenth century Chicago, tulip bulbs in seventeenth century Amsterdam), have long been essential elements of international trade. Such contracts were agreements between individual traders detailing the obligation (in the case of futures) or merely the right (in the case of options) to buy or sell a particular commodity at a given price either at, or at any time before, some point in the future. And though the movement of prices could obviously cause such contracts to become more valuable to their holders, this gain in value could only be realised by closing the original deal. In other words, such contracts were not liquid or liquifiable assets in their own right: they were not priced, they could be negotiated but not bought and sold in a market. And it is precisely this, the ability to trade them, to buy and sell them in a secondary financial market, that makes present-day *traded* financial futures/options not only a new and far-reaching monetary instrument, but also the means through which money – xenomoney – establishes itself as a sign able to signify its own future.

A traded option is a double object: a commodity which is bought and sold which itself promises to buy or sell some other commodity. The proclaimed point of options, their financial legitimation, is that they are instruments that create a form of insurance, a means of hedging against and managing risk. A trader holding commodity X is exposed to a loss if the price of X falls. The trader buys an option which gives him the right to sell X at current price at any time in next three months. If the price of X goes down, then the value at which such an option can be traded goes up thus the trader recoups the loss in holding X. If the price of X goes up, the option will have provided a hedge against an unrealised risk and its value will diminish to zero at the end of three months. But the same mechanism that is proclaimed as insurance can, and certainly does, function as speculation. There is of course nothing to prevent a trader who does not hold nor ever intends to hold X from buying such an option and gambling on a fall in the price of X to be able to sell the option at a profit.

Whether a form of insurance or speculation (the difference is unreal and for the present purposes irrelevant), options/futures trading has grown at a near vertical rate since the early 1970s, since, in fact, money became inconvertible and exchange rates floated against each other. Trade in them is now an essential and uneliminable component of the world money market (see Illustration 22).

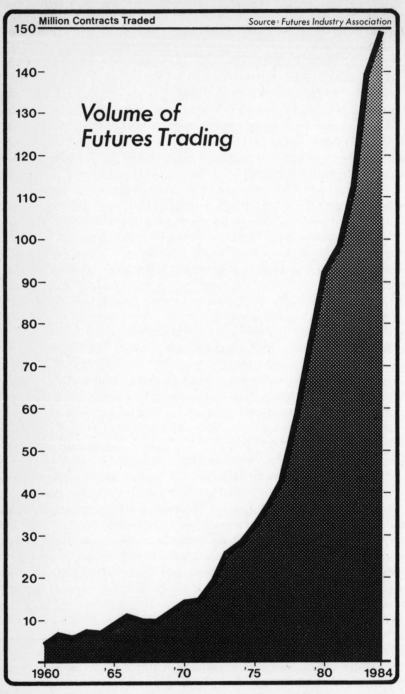

Illustration 22   Volume of futures trading, 1960–84.

What, then, is this multi-billion dollar a day market doing? What purposes is it serving? The conventional view of money, as the medium of exchange for goods, would have to answer that the billions flow in the service of world trade, that they finance transactions in goods and services. But few commentators would maintain this, and some version of the following seems generally accepted: 'Less than five per cent, perhaps only one or two per cent, of the tens of billions traded on the currency markets each day mirror an equivalent transaction in goods or services' (Stephens, 1985a). The rest of these tens of billions – the bulk – must therefore make up the secondary money market; a market devoted to the buying and selling of money and of futures/options on money. The significance of this is that the conventional vector of cause and necessity which points from trade to finance, from things to money, has been reversed: it is the financial tail that wags the dog of economy and trade:

The divorce between foreign exchange transactions and the trade flows which used to be their raison d'etre has resulted in an underlying volatility which ensures a steady turnover in expansion. The markets are now driven by capital rather than trade flows, and currencies have become commodities whose value depends more on the buyer's expectation of its resale value than on underlying economic developments.

(Stephens, 1985b)

This overturning of traditional causality, whereby the dynamics of purely monetary events influences the course of world trade rather than the reverse, where the epi-phenomenon and phenomenon are interchanged, is, in terms of signs, very familiar. It is the result of what has persistently presented itself as the loss of anteriority. As soon as the category of goods and commodities, with respect to which 'money' acts as a posterior medium of exchange, contains *that* money itself as a commodity, the distinction between prior 'things' and signs or tokens for these things disappears. And it only reappears, irrevocably altered, in the relation between signs and meta-signs. Money is always a sign, certainly when it is a medium, but also when it is a 'thing', a commodity, being bought and sold. The duality here is an inherent feature of money used to buy and sell itself. But it has a special character in the case of xenomoney because such money, being floating and inconvertible, is forced as a sign to create its own significance: one which is written in the only terms available to it, namely future states of itself. Xenomoney is thus a certain kind of meta-sign. Recall that the scandal of paper money for its detractors was its ability to increase the supply of money, in effect to create unlimited money, at the same time as the promise that it carried, to deliver palpable, uncreatable specie, denied this possiblity. Xenomoney, by making no promise to deliver anything, avoids such double dealing. Its scandal, if such exists, is the fact that it is a sign which creates itself out of the future.

This reflexivity of xenomoney is already implied by its independence, that is money governed by purely financial dynamics, from the physically determined constraints of underlying trade. Since what is implied by the separation of finance from so-called real trade is that any particular future state of money when it arrives will not be something 'objective', a referent waiting out there, determined by 'real' trade forces, but will have been brought into being by the very money-market activity designed to predict its value. The strategies provided by options and futures for speculation and insurance against money loss caused by volatility of exchange and interest rates become an inextricable part of what determines these rates.

Those antagonistic to xeonomoney take this last point to its causative limit and assert the following. Insurance against volatility through a multi-billion dollar futures/options market is directly and inevitably responsible for further volatlity; this in turn will be insured against, thus causing further volatility, and so on in an increasingly unstable spiral. If the xeno part of xenomoney threatened collapse of the world money system from the past, from unsupportable debt generated within the Euromarket, then the money part of it threatens, on this hostile view, a world monetary collapse from the future, from an unsustainable mutability of money signs created by the financial futures markets. Thus xeonomoney, to those convinced that it is not 'real' money but a dangerously unstable kind of pseudo-money, will either be drowned in the debt weight of its past or burned up in vertiginous and anarchic volatility derived from its future.

The semiotic shift in money signs from gold-backed paper money to xenomoney replicates and finalises the earlier move from gold itself to imaginary money. The emergence of xenomoney, in other words, signals the absolute exclusion of gold from the economic code, the final form of the relative and merely temporary severance between money signs and gold initiated by the institution of imaginary money. This exclusion is, as we have seen, fundamental: it is the loss of transcendental origin, the end of a 'grounding' of money signs in some natural thing imagined to have a pre-monetary worth; the necessary absence of any intrinsic iconic value which supposedly precedes the money signs defined in relation to it. Semiotically such a termination corresponds precisely to the loss of anteriority which zero achieves in relation to number signs. Recall that by drawing attention to the failure of the anteriority of things to signs in the case of itself (what possible prior 'thing' can it be referring to?) zero demolishes the illusion of anteriority for *all* numbers. Once zero enters the scene numbers can no longer be paraded (however much they can be practically considered so, which is an entirely different question) as aggregations of some exterior, pre-numerical 'unit' which serves as their prior, definitional origin, but must instead be considered, as Stevin so pentratingly saw, to be elements of a system *created* by zero; or rather, created by the counting subject whose presence as a signifying agency zero witnesses. In short, zero numeralises the 'unit' as xenomoney commodities gold: a process whereby gold and the unit lose their claim to be transcendental origins and become rewritten and unremarkable as just signs within their respective systems.

THE 'TEXT'

The status of language, the nature of the signifying limits and possibilities of spoken and written signs within late twentieth-century philosophical and literary discussion is a fought-over terrain – problematic, undecided, and contentiously indeterminate. Language is said to be corrupted by metaphysics, opaque to its own incoherence, to be in crisis, to display symptoms of frenetic unbalance and hyperactivity, to live under a false and self-sustaining image, and to be incapable of offering, this side of silence, any description of itself that is not implicated and immediately nullified by what is 'described'. What, if there is a problem, is its source? *Is* language in a state of sickness, deluded and blind to its own imprisonment? Where, supposing that to be the case is the way out, the solution? The philosopher Jacques Derrida, responsible more than any contemporary figure for insistently articulating and diagnosing the 'problem' of language, locates the recognition of it (which of course dictates what a 'solution' if any would be) at the extreme boundary of Western rational thought, on the horizon of Occidental metaphysics:

However the topic is considered, the *problem of language* has never been simply one problem among others. But never as much as at present has it invaded, *as such*, the global horizon of the most diverse researches and the most heterogeneous discourses, diverse in their intention, method, and ideology. The devaluation of the world 'language' itself, and how, in the very hold it has upon us, it betrays a loose vocabulary, the temptation of a cheap seduction, the passive yielding to fashion, the consciousness of the avant-garde, in other words – ignorance – are evidence of this effect. The inflation of the sign 'language' is the inflation of the sign itself, absolute inflation, inflation itself. Yet by one of its aspects or shadows, it is itself a sign: this crisis is also a symptom. It indicates, as if in spite of itself, that a historico-metaphysical epoch *must* finally determine as language the totality of its problematic horizon. It must do so not only because all that desire had wished to wrest from the play of language finds itself recaptured within that play but also because, for the same reason, language itself is menaced in its very life, helpless, adrift in the threat of limitlessness, brought back to its own finitude at the very moment when its limits seem to disappear, when it ceases to be self-assured, contained, and guaranteed by the infinite signified which seemed to exceed it.

(Derrida, 1976, p. 6)

Thus Derrida, writing at the beginning of the 'The End of the Book and the Beginning of Writing', which begins his own book, *Of Grammatology*, whose purpose is to demonstrate that there is no beginning, origin, first being, initial presence within the world of language and written signs. Derrida proposes a whole new order of the 'text', of what is meant by saying that something is a text, an interpretable piece of 'writing'; an order intended to negate, overturn, unmask the illusion of what he calls *logocentrism*: the metaphysical belief that writing is a secondary, posterior activity, an activity that comes after, represents, transcribes, is a sign of other necessarily prior signs. These signs possess the special 'presence', the originating self-confirming palpability, the fullness of 'hearing (understanding)-oneself-speak' that is accorded traditionally but falsely to the logos, to *spoken* language (Derrida, 1976, p. 7).

What for Derrida sustains the traditional and misguided account of the opposition speech/writing, allowing writing to be characterised in terms of its secondarity, as the transcription of psychologically and epistemologically prior speaking, is the parallel acceptance of a whole series of oppositions – identity/difference, presence/absence, reality/image, thing/sign, literal/metaphorical – basic to Western conceptions of the linguistic sign. In each of these oppositional categories there is assumed to be a degree zero: one of the terms is privileged as original, generic, and primary, the other subsidiary and specified in relation to it. Thus difference is the lack of a priorly conceived identity, absence is non-existence of a primary presence, images represent a given and already existent reality, signs are tokens of pre-signifying 'things' which precede them, the metaphorical is a species of the more fundamental category of the non-literal.
non-literal.

Derrida's thesis is that all such binary orderings are misplaced and illusory and that the priorities they take for granted must be dismantled and overturned. His strategy is to *deconstruct* each of these oppositions, to read texts depending on and structured around them, and show, through a certain mode of textual attention, that what at first appears as the privileged originating term is as secondary and dependent as the minor term it supposedly gives rise to. The category of literal is incoherent except in relation to the figurative, the idea of presence cannot be explicated except in terms of absence, what we call reality is already permeated by so-called representations, talk of 'things' cannot be rationally mounted except in terms of signs (of things). Such a deconstructive programme is to be achieved through a kind of anti-reading, a reading of texts against themselves, an interpretive activity which, much like psychoanalytic listening, ignores the text's own protocols of reading, its preferred, official, ostensive, declared modes of interpretation, in favour of what is not said nor intended to be said through these oppositions. In the significance of the text's silences, gaps, hidden denials and disavowals, in its excesses and circumlocutions, in the breaks and continuities of its narrative, in what the text avoids and what it insists on, in its apparently 'neutral' choices of metaphor, and so on.

To understand what is meant by and what is at stake in the process of 'deconstruction' it would be natural, then, to explicate it, and with it Derrida's notion of the 'text', through a description and replay of his readings. I shall not do this, but instead adopt a different procedure, and focus as Derrida himself might advocate on the metaphors he himself uses in the passage quoted above. He speaks of 'devaluation' and 'inflation' of the sign. These are of course monetary terms describing the ways a currency loses its value in relation to other currencies and in relation to itself. If his gloss on 'devaluation' – loose vocabulary, cheap seduction, passive yielding to fashion, avant-garde and ignorance – makes it no more significant, perhaps, than a passing swipe at the *demi-monde* of cafe intellectualism, the same cannot be said of 'inflation'. Its obsessive and impacted repetition, equating inflation of 'language' with inflation of linguistic signs with inflation itself, seems to telescope the text into itself in a way that asks for elaboration. Inflation occurs when money is worth less than it was; it indicates that the relation between money signs and what they signify – value – is put into question and, if continued, threatened with a dissolution in which ultimately money becomes worthless. Now the 'value' of a written sign, in the present case a text, is presumably the signified of the sign, what the text means or can be made to mean. But since it is precisely the notion of a text's 'meaning' that the Derrida programme has to interrogate, his monetary image seems to blow itself up. The metaphor of inflation seems itself inflationary as it spirals from language to the sign to absolute inflation to 'inflation itself'.

Faced with this sort of vertigo, and mindful of Derrida's own scheme to dismantle the figurative/literal opposition, let us be simple-mindedly 'literal' and agree to dissolve the distinction between money and writing: treat texts, interpretable results of writing, as if they were *circulating money signs*, and look at money signs as *pieces of writing*. We might ask, for example, what in the world of the text corresponds to – 'literally' *is* – paper money? Or, where in the field of money signs does logocentrism, that is the metaphysical belief that signs are always grounded in some ultimate originating beginning experienced as a full, self-validating presence, make its appearance? Thus Derrida's tracing of the metaphysics of presence back some twenty-five centuries to the pre-Socratic philosophers, becomes, within our assumed literalness, an equivalent dating back to Croesus, to the sixth century BC Lydian invention of circulating *gold* money. In which case the myth of presence gold gave to money signs, that is the origin of value, the source of transcendental 'intrinsic' worth, the value in kind (specie) and not token, the preciousness incarnate and palpably present, finds its image in, and in fact is, the logocentric fantasy of an originating transcendantal presence behind written signs.

For money signs the resting place of this myth, as we saw, was convertible paper money. The US Treasury, by promising the bearer of a dollar redemption in gold, located the absolute value and origin of its money-signs in a material, physical presence stored in Fort Knox. How and in what sense are texts convertible or inconvertible? What sort of redemption does the convertible written sign, which we might call the *paper text*, promise? Paper texts are a medium of exchange for 'real' items; tokens for goods and services that are physical and palpable; signs standing in place of what can be experienced, consumed, made present; secondary vehicles representing an original presentation, delivering a direct, tangible immersion in some world of experience before signs. They point to, indicate, and refer to this world, outside themselves and the order of signs they constitute, for their authenticity and validation. They are convertible into what this world determines to be 'reality'. The specie they promise to deliver is the icon of pure speech, meaning-originating speech, speech that is unmediated, filled, pre-semiotic, real to itself *without the agency of signs*. And the signified of these texts, their monetary value, is a 'meaning', some determinate entity that issues from the supposedly referential relation between the signs of the text and events in this pre-signified originating world.

But what if the existence of such a world is an illusion? What if there is no world before signs, no ultimate presence, no pre-semiotic speech, no possibility of specie, no redemption by gold, no grounding of signs in an origin, no intrinsic self-signifying icon of value? If all signs owe their being to, and are necessarily preceded by, other signs, if the signs are *in principle* inconvertible into non-signs,if the promise to deliver specie is necessarily void, then paper texts cease to be what they claim – secondary tokens representing a prior world – and become instead items in a world from which signs can never be absent. If such is the case, then what they took to be their 'meaning', to be delivered up as a relation to that signless world, becomes a phantom, a reification of an illusory presence. In short, paper texts would cease to 'mean' in the sense they themselves give to this term: they would not be able to be redeemed in terms more original, more 'present', more palpably 'real' than themselves: they would therefore be signs in a state of unacknowledged and irreparable dislocation from what they take to be their signifieds.

Such, as we saw, was the fate of paper-money signs from the point when the US dollar ceased to be convertible into precious metal. And such is Derrida's account of the status of the logocentric text as a form and practice of writing blind to the possibility of any reading of itself that would release it from its metaphysical attachment to presence. Paper-money signs were replaced, usurped by those of xenomoney, and a new world order of money signs came into being. What replaces the paper text? What would the order of linguistic signs appropriate to such a *xenotext* look like? Can it be equated with that of the deconstructed text, with Derrida's conception of writing conscious of the secondarity of all linguistic signs? What would be the protocols for reading such writing? Where would what it signifies come from? What is there, gold and originating presence having been repudiated, to guarantee that a xenotext *has* any significance?

For xenomoney the answer, as we saw, was brutally simple: it guarantees itself. Or rather it ceases to offer 'guarantees' outside itself. Divorced by fiat from any source of 'intrinsic' value outside its own universe of signs, it is forced as a sign to engage in the creation of its own signified – one written in the only terms available to it, that is future states of itself. By buying and selling itself through time, that is commoditising the difference between its spot and forward values, xenomoney achieves a certain sort of self-creation. It is a time-bound sign that scandalously manufactures its own signified, what it insists is its value, as it goes along.

Now the problem of linguistic value, what it is and should be, is not new. Saussure long ago insisted on the necessary absence in relation to language of any intrinsically valued, extra-lingual item which was supposed to serve as an origin for the meaning of a sign. On the contrary, it was essential, he argued, to give a purely structuralist account of the value of signs, one encapsulated in his slogan that there are no positive terms in language but only differences, that the meaning of a sign lies in and can only lie in its relations of identity and difference with other signs. But in Saussure there is still the primacy of speech. It is spoken language, the sign system that purports to directly transmit thoughts, ideas, signifieds from the mind of one speaker to another (as opposed to writing which inscribes such speech) that is the place of differentiation. But if, as Derrida claims, speech is subject to the same secondarity traditionally the preserve of writing, if speech is a sign of a sign, then Saussure's structuralism is inadequate, and a more complex notion that difference is required, conceived as it is in terms of opposition to the prior category of identity and buttressed by the parallel priority within the opposition speech/writing. This more complex principle of signification Derrida neologises in French as 'differance' to convey the sense of *deferrence*, spacing, postponement, placing into the future, that necessarily lies behind and within any difference. Unlike Saussure's 'difference', Derrida's deferrence is not locatable in the supposed primacy of speech; it recognises difference as a secondary phenomenon. Difference is the trace of other semiotically *prior* differentiation. The temporal element that deferrence has to convey cannot then be confined to the purely static, geometric structuralism governing difference within Saussure's theoretical linguistic space. It indicates, in other words, an event, a *creation in time*.

What is the effect of deferrence at the level of interpretable writing: how does the signified of a text in Derrida's story of writing postpone itself? Answer: by becoming a time-bound sign which continually manufactures – just as xenomoney, faced with the loss of gold's intrinsic presence, is obliged to manufacture – a signfied, a value, from the possibilities of its own future.

Paper texts point backwards: they offer to deliver that which has been deposited, something buried in a vault in the past. Their value stems from the promise of this redemption, the possibility of retrieving at least in principle some original full self-affirming 'meaning'. The xenotext offers no redemption, no written promise of hidden treasure, no icon of value, no delivery of some precious, proto-signifying, specie. What was a past meaning, waiting intact and whole to be claimed, independent of the act of retrieving it, is displaced by a de-mythologised future significance, fractured, open and inherently plural. For the xenotext there is nothing to *retrieve*; there is only language in a state of potential and never actualised interpretation. What it signifies is its capacity to further signify. Its value is determined by its ability to bring readings of itself into being. A xenotext thus has no ultimate 'meaning', no single, canonical, definitive, or final 'interpretation': it has a signified only to the extent that it can be made to engage in the process of creating an inter-pretive future for itself. It 'means' what its interpreters cannot prevent it from meaning.

Postponing meaning into the future has the result of displacing the text into a foreign off-shore version of its previous, paper, self. The yet to be deconstructed domestic version, which is seen as insisting on a reading within its own sovereignty, within the orbit of its declared 'natural' inter-pretation, becomes as soon as it is read against and through itself alien, a foreign sign de-centered from the logos and all the self-confirmation it finds there: what was 'difference' in the presence dominated conception of the text is displaced into the xenotext's 'defference', what was self-present speech becomes reinterpreted and reconceived as a 'writing' in which all signs are already signs of other signs, and so on.

But if Derrida writes of signs acquiring a fully fledged secondarity, of signifiers being already signifieds as soon as they 'enter the game' of language being played against itself, one cannot, however, interpret either the establishment or practice of xenowriting in the absence of the writing which gives rise to it. For like the Eurodollar, which is both host and parasite on the dollar, the xenotext can displace but never entirely substitute for the domestic sign it appears to repudiate. In the market where the game of texts is played, the semiosis of writing in relation to itself occurs through a circula-tion of texts which are at once objects and medium of exchange: commentary and text, writing and writing about writing, literature and criticism, become no longer distinguishable as opposed and separate categories. Neither can claim any autonomy from the other, and those who write texts abut a text by reading it against itself, can be seen to enact and thereby perpetuate on the level of interpretation the very secondary of writing which their readings insist upon uncovering. Like authors of futures contracts, market players whose predictive speculations about the future value of the money commodity they trade are perpetually in danger of being instruments which bring this value into being, deconstructive readers produce strategies of reading that operate through the fiction that the results of their readings are somehow independent of the interpretive presumptions and manner of their production.

What this means is that *text* in Derrida's account of 'writing' exhibits precisely the principal semiotic characteristics of xenomoney within financial capitalism: it marks a new order of inconvertible, floating, futured, off-shore signs.

It is worth mentioning at this point a related, but less synchronically based, homology to the structure of present-day money signs. Thus, there is undoubtedly a parallel between the order of signs constituted by xenomoney as given here and the order of the 'pure simulacrum' described by Baudrillard in his essay *The Precession of Simulacra*. Specifically, one can map the diachronic stages of money, (i) gold, (ii) imaginary, (iii) paper, (iv) xeno, on to the 'successive phases of the image' of some 'basic reality' in so far as the image, (i) is a 'reflection' of this reality, (ii) 'masks and perverts this reality', (iii) 'marks the absence of this reality', (iv) 'bears no relation to this reality . . . and is its own pure simulacrum' (1983, p. 11). Unfortunately, Baudrillard's seductive insistence that the 'real' has finally become precisely what can be simulated is too totalised and his characterisation of 'images' too amorphous for one to be able to determine what, for example, would follow from the claim that xenomoney is (or indeed is not) its own pure simulacrum.

The semiotic connection between money and Derrida's notion of writing on the other hand is by no means so nebulous. Within their respective domains, in the codes of writing and money, 'text' and xenomoney function as cognate meta-signs. Each appears on the scene as a denial of anteriority, the negation of the transcendant value that underpins the code it disrupts. Derrida's repudiation of an 'origin', of an 'infinite signified' which exceeds language, destabilises the possibility of a text having a 'canonical' privileged meaning in precisely the same way that financial capitalism's reduction of gold to a commodity among commodities contradicts the possibility of money having an 'intrinsic' privileged value. And if, for its opponents, xenomoney moves always on the edge of total monetary chaos, it is no less so that, to its detractors and critics, deconstructionism pushes writing ever nearer to senseless vacuity.

Articulating a structural morphism of this sort justifies giving an artificially 'literal' reading of Derrida's metaphor, if that is what it is, of infla-tion. But if my treatment of his thesis (squinting at it in a mirror which reflects only monetary images) produces a grotesque metonym, a cartoon reading of his attack on Occidental metaphysics (for after all, writing is not transacting, speech is other than buying and selling, linguistic signs admit infinitely more subtle, multi-dimensional, rich, diverse, *conscious*, and universal interpretations than those of money) it none the less assumes a particular interest in relation to the signifying structures explored in the present essay.

This is because, on the one hand, the existence of connections, morphisms, and parallelisms between monetary value and textual meaning is hardly unexpected. As Mauss (1969) in his essay, *The Gift*, famously demonstrated, they both can be seen to emerge from much older archaicly structured circulations of cultural meanings centred on the forms of exchange governing honour, duty, obligation, and so on, which antedate the invention of textual writing – 'Men could pledge their honour long before they could sign their names' – as well as the use of money-signs (Mauss, 1969, p. 36). Indeed, the parallelism between the circulation of meaning and money is so long standing and rooted in common usage that the metaphors which express it, including 'bankrupt' points of view, words being 'coined', 'spent' meanings, 'inflated' and 'devalued' ideas, intellectual 'debts', have all but lost their imagistic power. Moreover, the simultaneous emergence of a new form of money and a new form of textual writing which, so I have argued, share a common semiotic explication can be seen as a fresh extension of the parallelism; an extension that could be further elaborated by identifying the new, still imagistically alive, textual homomorphs of option contracts, credit risk, volatility, ultimate lender and the like.

On the other hand, what *is* unexpected is the re-emergence, within Derrida's account of linguistic signs, of the same semiotic mechanism and matrix of formal connections, that is the emergence of a meta-sign whose disruption is precisely the loss of a transcendental origin and with it the loss of anteriority, first identified for the mathematical sign zero.

Unexpected, and unlooked for, for the following reason: the entire analysis of zero presented earlier in this book is given within what might be called a pre-theoretical undeconstructed vocabulary and is, presumably, therefore riddled with and invalidated by the very metaphysics of 'presence' it is being used to characterise. The semiotic formula given of zero, that is a sign for the absence of other signs, not only works from a rudimentary and theoretically simple reading of 'sign' as a signifier/signified coupling, an event, thing, gesture which is accorded significance by a subject, but more importantly explicitly invokes and indeed *constitutes itself* in terms of the logocentrically tainted opposition of absence/presence. Furthermore, contrary to the whole persuasion of Derrida's thesis that origins are always mythical and looking for origins of signs is the central illusion of Western metaphysics, zero is depicted here as a sign which, though it demolishes the anteriority inherent in the idea of an absolute and transcendental origin, is nevertheless itself *nothing other than an origin.* Again, in order to talk of zero as a *meta*-sign, a sign about the absence/presence of other signs, it is necessary to ascribe to zero a secondarity denied, necessarily, to these other signs. One must, in other words, reject the idea that the inherent secondarity of all signs (their signifiers always being signifieds of other signs) implies that some signs cannot, like zero, be more signs of signs, more secondary, literally more significant, than others. And finally, the very function which zero enjoys within mathematics as the mark of an origin requires there to be, as we saw, a certain sort of subject present, a conscious intentional agency, whose 'presence' at the initiation of the process of counting is precisely what zero signifies.

To present matters in such a way is in no sense to suggest that by being undeconstructed our account of zero must be illusory. Rather it is to point out, as a final gloss on the 'text' here, that deconstructivism is a species of global absolutism which, in the end, does not impinge on a text which claims no more for its oppositions than that they are local and relative. Thus Derrida's arguments tell us that there is no *absolute* origin to signs (signs are always already there) that there is no *absolute* category of meta-sign (all signs are meta-signs since they refer to and invoke other signs) that there is no *absolute* sense of the literal (what is figurative and non-figurative interpenetrate) that there is no *absolute* signifier (signifiers cannot but be signifieds of other signs, and so on). But there is in these denials no reason why a sign such as zero cannot be a *relative* origin, why zero cannot signify absence relative to the presence of certain signs, why, that is, zero cannot be privileged as a meta-sign with respect to other signs not so privileged.

Observe, finally, that zero is an origin at a very primitive, parsimonious and minimally articulated, level of sign formation. Signification codes difference, hence the need for more than one sign. How to produce, with the minimum of *ad hoc* extra-semiotic means, two 'different' signs? Answer: let there be a sign – call it 1 – and let there be another sign – call it 0 – indicating the absence of the sign 1. Of course, such a procedure *produces* the difference it appears subsequently to describe; and the use of absence to manufacture difference in this way is a viable sign practice only through the simultaneous introduction of a syntax: a system of placing signifiers in linear relation to each other in such a way that it allows signs to be interpretable in terms of the original absence/presence signified by 0.

The sign 1 can be anything. If 1 is one and 0 is zero and the syntax is the standard positional notation for numbers, then what results, as the limiting case of the system, is the two-valued descendant of the Hindu decimal system. Leibniz, who spent much time formulating the rules for binary arithmetic, was deeply impressed by the generative, infinitely proliferative principle inherent in such zero-based binarism: so much so that he refracted the binary relation between 1 and 0 into an iconic image for the Old Testament account of creation *ex nihilo*, whereby the universe (the infinitude of

Illustration 23   Title page of *Mathematical Proof of the Creation and Ordering of the World* by Leibniz, 1734.

numbers) is created by God (the unbroken 1) from the void (the cypher 0) (see Illustration 23).

Again, if 1 signifies the presence of a current in a circuit and 0 signifies the absence of such a current and the syntax is 2-valued Boolean algebra, then what emerges is the binary formalism within which the logic and language of all present-day computer programs are ultimately written. Thus, to pursue zero further, would be to have to say more about its role at the origin of this formalism. But such a project would require a critique of mathematical logic. In particular, one would need to unravel the assumptions behind the claim that is made for Boolean logic, with its referential apparatus of truth and falsity, to be *the* grammar of all mathematical, hence all scientifico-technical, hence all supposedly neutral, culturally invariant, objective, true/false assertions about some prior 'real' world. To do this would require a semiotics that went beyond zero to the whole field of mathematical discourse. A semiotics which, in order to begin at all, would have to demolish the widely held metaphysical belief that mathematical signs point to, refer to, or invoke some world, some supposedly objective eternal domain, other than that of their own human, that is time bound, changeable, subjective and finite making.

Bibliography

ALPERS, S. *The Art of Describing* (John Murray, London, 1983).

ANGELL, N. *The Story of Money* (Cassell, London, 1930).

AUGUSTINE, ST. *Confessions*, trans. Pine-Coffin (Penguin, London, 1961).

BANNOCK, G., R. BAXTER and R. REES, *Dictionary of Economics* (Penguin, London, 1984).

BAUDRILLARD, J. *The Precession of Simulacra*, P. Foss, P. Potter and P. Beitchmun trans. (Semiotext(e), New York, 1983).

BAXANDALL, M. *Painting and Experience in 15th Century Italy* (Clarendon, Oxford, 1972).

BLOOM, H. *Kabbalah and Criticism* (The Seabury Press, New York, 1975).

BRAUDEL, F. *Capitalism and Modern Life, 1400–1800* (Fontana, London, 1974).

BRYSON, N. *Vision and Painting: the Logic of the Gaze* (Macmillan, London, 1983).

COLIE, R. *Paradoxia Epidemica* (Princeton University Press, Princeton, 1966).

CULLER, J. *The Pursuit of Signs* (Routledge & Kegan Paul, London, 1981).

CUSA, N. de *The Vision of God or the Icon*, N. Salter (trans.) (Dent, London, 1928).

DAVIDSON, J. *Eurodollars, the Currency without a Country* (Reader's Digest, May, 1983).

DERRIDA, J. *Of Grammatology*, G. C. Spivak (trans.) (Johns Hopkins University Press, Baltimore, 1976).

EDGERTON, S. *The Renaissance Rediscovery of Linear Perspective* (Harper & Row, New York, 1976).

FREGE, G. *The Foundations of Arithmetic*, J. L. Austin (trans.) (Blackwell, Oxford, 1974).

FOUCAULT, M. *The Order of Things* (Vantage Books, New York, 1973).

GALBRAITH, K. *Money: Whence it Came, Where it Went* (Andre Deutsch, London, 1975).

GOMBRICH, E. *Meditations on a Hobby Horse* (Phaidon, London, 1963).

GRIBBLE, C. *Studies Presented to R. Jakobson* (Slavica, Cambridge, Mass., 1968).

GRAHAM, W. *The One Pound Note in the History of Banking in Great Britain* (James Thin, Edinburgh, 1911).

HOGAN, W. and PEARCE, I. *The Incredible Eurodollar* (Allen & Unwin, London, 1984).

KIRK, G. and RAVEN, J. *The Presocratic Philosophers* (Cambridge University Press, Cambridge, 1957).

KLEIN, J. *Greek Mathematical Thought and The Origin of Algebra*, E. Brann (trans.) (MIT Press, Cambridge, Mass., 1968).

MAUSS, M. *The Gift*, Cunnison (trans.) (Routledge & Kegan Paul, London, 1969).

MILLER, J. A. 'Suture (elements of the logic of the signifier)', *Screen*, Winter, 1977–78.

MONTAIGNE, M. *Essays*, J. Florio (trans.) (Stott, London, 1889).

NEEDHAM, J. *Science and Civilisation in China, Vol. III* (Cambridge University Press, Cambridge, 1959).

NISHITANI, K. *Religion and Nothingness*, J. Van Bragt (trans.) (University of California Press, 1982).

PULLAN, J. M. *The History of the Abacus* (Hutchinson, London, 1968).

RICE, E. *The Adding Machine* (Samuel French, New York, 1956).

RIDER, F. *The Dialectic of Selfhood in Montaigne* (Stanford University Press, Stanford, 1973).

ROTMAN, B. 'Towards a Semiotics of Mathematics', *Semiotica* (in press).

SAYCE, R. *The Essays of Montaigne* (Weidenfeld & Nicolson, London, 1972).

SCHOLEM, G. *Major Trends in Jewish Mysticism* (Schocken, Jerusalem, 1941).

SHAKESPEARE, W. *King Lear* (Methuen, London, 1969).

SHELL, M. 'The Gold Bug', *Genre*, vol. XIII, pp. 11–30, 1980.

SMITH, A. *An Inquiry into the Nature and Causes of the Wealth of Nations* (Clarendon Press, Oxford, 1976).

SNYDER, J. '*Las Meninas* and the Mirror of the Prince', *Critical Inquiry*, vol. 11, pp. 539–72, 1985.

STEPHENS, P. *Financial Times Surveys*, 18 June, London, 1985a.

STEPHENS, P. *Financial Times Surveys*, 16 September, London, 1985b.

STEVIN, S. P. *The Principal Works of Simon Stevin* (Swets & Zeitlinger, Amsterdam, 1958).

UNAMUNO, M. de *The Tragic Sense of Life* Kerrigan (trans.), A. Kerrigan and M. Nozick (eds) (Princeton University Press, Princeton, 1972).

VRIES, Jan V. de *Perspective* (Dover Publications, New York, 1968).

WEYL, H. *Philosophy of Mathematics and Natural Science* (Princeton University Press, Princeton, 1949).

WILDEN, A. *System and Structure: Essays in Communication and Exchange* (Harper & Row, New York, 1972).

Index